D0050031

Dr. Samuel Lee has a dynamic testimony of how he came to Christ through the prayers of his wife and through his personal encounter with Jesus. I recommend his biography to everyone wanting to learn more about the stimulating challenge of being a soldier of the cross!
—*Dr. David Yonggi Cho, Senior Pastor*
Yoido Full Gospel Church
Korea

30/11/2015

"Escribe al ángel de la
iglesia en Filadelfia:
Esto dice el Santo, el verdadero,
el que tiene la llave de David,
el que abre y ninguno cierra, y
cierra y ninguno abre:

Yo conozco tus obras; he aquí
he puesto delante de ti una
puerta abierta, la cual nadie
puede cerrar, porque aunque
tienes poca fuerza, has
guardado mi palabra, y no
has negado mi nombre."

Apocalipsis 3:7-8

"Porque escrito está: Vivo yo, dice el
Señor, que ante mí se doblará toda
rodilla, y toda lengua confesará a Dios."
Romanos 14:11

SOLDIER of the CROSS

Samuel Lee

CREATION
HOUSE
PRESS

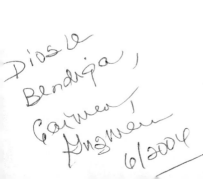

SOLDIER OF THE CROSS BY DR. SAMUEL LEE
Published by Creation House Press
A part of Strang Communications Company
600 Rinehart Road
Lake Mary, Florida 32746
www.creationhouse.com

Unless otherwise noted, all Scripture quotations are from the Holy
Bible, New International Version. Copyright © 1973, 1978, 1984,
International Bible Society. Used by permission.

Scripture quotations marked NKJV are from the New King James
Version of the Bible. Copyright © 1979, 1980, 1982 by Thomas
Nelson, Inc., publishers. Used by permission.

Scripture quotations marked KJV are from the King James Version of
the Bible.

Library of Congress Catalog Card Number: 00-111323
International Standard Book Number: 0-88419-762-X (paperback)

1 2 3 4 5 6 7 BP 8 7 6 5 4 3 2 1
Printed in the United States of America

Dedication

This book is dedicated to
my dearest friend and partner,
THE HOLY SPIRIT,
Who is the fountain of my inspirations
and my existence in the path of life.

Thanks!

Acknowledgments

To my wife, Sarah, who led me to Christ.

And to my beloved sons,
David and Jonathan,
the colors of my life.

Contents

Foreword

THE POWER OF SAMUEL LEE'S BOOK, *SOLDIER OF THE Cross,* which you are about to read, is drawn from what we call the "power of a testimony." An argument or an opinion is no match for this kind of power, for indeed, an honest testimony of a changed life stands by itself, needing no props.

The irresistible effect of Christ's disciples has always emanated from the power of their testimony. Transformation, energized by the Holy Spirit, produces not only lasting change but undeniable authenticity. Honest testimonies "ring true" to the saved and unsaved alike. Samuel's life experiences, so openly shared with us here, have the sound of truth. His life in Christ is not only real for him, it is contagious when one encounters it.

Whether you have walked as a believer for years or have just begun to ponder Christ's claim on your life, Samuel's experiences and lessons from the Master will bring you insight, joy and renewed motivation. May the Lord continue to open new doors for you as you take this journey with Samuel. And may the King and His kingdom continue to grow through us all—as we respond to God's heart, and as God responds to the needs of an increasingly desperate world.

—DENNIS T. PEACOCKE
PRESIDENT, STRATEGIC CHRISTIAN SERVICES
SANTA ROSA, CALIFORNIA

Chapter 1

The Plastic Cross

LIFE IN THE LORD IS A JOURNEY. WHILE HIS PATHWAY IS full of challenges, it is an exodus into a victorious life. My own journey began when I was born in the Middle East. I grew up in a Muslim country where the values are quite different from those of the average westerner. I remember having a great fear of God. I grew up hearing stories of Abraham, Isaac and Jacob; but, of course, they were the Islamic versions of them! It may be hard for you to understand this, but I have always loved the God that I knew at that time.

WHO IS THAT?

My interest in Jesus began when I was just six years old. It was just an ordinary day, but something extraordinary was about to happen. I was sitting next to my father as he slowly drove along one of the busy streets of my hometown. It was fun to see how people along the edge of the

1

roadway were selling fruits, vegetables, books, magazines, old newspapers and almost anything you could think of. To me, it seemed like you could buy almost anything there.

Then suddenly, something really grabbed my attention. My father was driving so slowly that I could look closely at the pictures an old man was selling. I was admiring one beautiful picture after another, when suddenly, one of the pictures took me by complete surprise. There before me was a picture of a half-naked Man hanging from a cross. His face was looking down as if He was crying. He was suffering, and somehow I could feel His agony and pain.

I quickly asked my dad, "Who is that?"

My father said, "Isa (Jesus) was crucified on the cross because people were mean to Him. He is a prophet of Allah, just like all other prophets."

Despite what my father said, seeing that picture did something to me. It moved me. In fact, I have never forgotten the picture of the cross on which that Man hung. At that time I could not grasp why the Man was suffering and crying. *Why did He suffer? Why did He hang from that cross? Who did that to Him?* These were questions I asked myself over and over.

God heard the cry of my heart, and just a year later my parents enrolled me in a Christian school. Although my family was Muslim, I could study at the school because it was a custom for boys from rich families to attend private schools. Fortunately for me, at that time private schools in my country were almost always Christian Orthodox or Catholic.

My journey to discover why that Man in the picture hung on the cross continued to unfold when I secretly ventured over to the big old church that towered in the middle of the school yard. Although local Christians worshiped there on Sundays, the church was closed during the week. One day my curiosity got the best of me and I sneaked over to peer through the church windows. There it was again. As I peeked inside the church, I saw a picture of that same Man. Again, He was hanging on a cross. Now my desire to know about this Man grew even more. Something was burning in me. I wanted to know more about Him.

God's guiding hand was clearly upon because I met a new friend at school who was an Orthodox Christian. I certainly do not think it was any coincidence that the very first friend I ever had was a Christian. He seemed like just the right person to ask about the Man hanging on the cross.

He answered, "He is Isa (Jesus), the Messiah." The Romans killed Him, he added.

His answer fueled my burning desire to know more and more about Jesus. In fact, I asked my seven-year-old friend many questions about Him. Then because I wanted to know even more, I started going to a bookshop to buy booklets about the story of Jesus. Although I enjoyed the colorful pictures and stories, it was hard for me to understand what they meant.

Then one day my little friend told me some amazing news. He said, "Jesus is not dead; He is alive, and He hears us even now as we speak." This was astounding news for me: "Jesus is alive!"

Conditions were about to radically change in my country, but before extremists came to power, God made sure that I learned about Jesus. When the extremists came to power, there was so much killing that it was like a bloodbath in my country. All Christian schools were closed down, and my bestfriend had to leave the country. During our last day together, my young friend told me that his family soon had to leave the country because his father believed that hard times were coming there for Christians.

Tears ran down my face and sadness captured my little heart as my friend told me that he and his family would have to go away and never come back again. Before my friend left me, he took the plastic cross hanging around his neck and gave it to me. He told me that I should not worry, because the cross would always remind me of him, and it would protect me any time I needed help. He left, and I never saw him again. Although he was gone, I still had my sweet memories of his friendship.

Even today, memories of his face, his words and that plastic cross continue to echo in my heart as sweet reminders of how, by God's goodness and grace, that seven-year-old friend planted the Seed in me! The plastic cross was very dear to me. In fact, until things changed in my country and my mother advised me that it was dangerous to wear the cross around my neck, I always kept it with me.

"Besides, we are not Christians," she told me.

After that, I never saw that plastic cross again. Either I lost it or my mom took it. Even though this challenged me, no one could take away the childlike love for Jesus that I had in my heart.

Circumstances changed dramatically during the civil war in my country. It was no longer easy to buy books about Jesus. One day I returned to the shop where I normally would buy booklets about Jesus. I asked the man there if he was still selling books and pictures of Jesus. The man became angry and said, "Hey! You are not a Christian. I cannot sell them to you."

I told him, "I swear to God I am a Christian." Because I lied, I was able to buy Christian books with nice pictures and secretly read them when I was in bed. Every night I would pray to Jesus and ask Him to protect me.

I found comfort in knowing that Jesus was still alive. I

knew this because my bestfriend had told me that Jesus rose from the dead, and He will come back one day to change the world!

No Freedom in My Country

My country was constantly changing; we had no more freedom. I had never seen so many soldiers in my life, except in the movies. The Christian schools closed down and many Christians left the country and fled to Europe or America.

I went to an Islamic high school where we studied the Koran and religion. One day during our religion class, we had a lesson on Christianity that was specifically about Jesus and the story of Mary. The lesson that day would shake my faith and break my heart. The teacher said that Jesus was a prophet, but somehow He could not finish the job of Allah properly. So, Mohammad came to fulfill what Jesus could not fulfill. He told us that Mohammad was the last prophet of God. He said that even Jesus had prophesied of Mohammad's coming!

Regarding Jesus' death, the teacher said Jesus had a disciple called Judas, who looked like Him. The Romans made a mistake in killing Judas instead of Jesus. This is why some disciples were fooling themselves when they thought they saw Jesus walking in the streets. They began to believe that Jesus had risen from the dead, which my teacher said was not true.

I believed my teacher, so in those few minutes, my inner world collapsed and crashed down. My tender heart was broken. I became angry with my friend because I thought he had lied to me. I was disappointed in Jesus and in all the stories I had read and heard as a child.

This devastation turned into rebellion. In fact, I turned

into an angry rebel during my teen years. I became interested in Islam and in the Koran. I even began to enjoy reading religious books about Islam, when just a few years earlier I had been sneaking to read books about Jesus.

My fascination with the Koran was short-lived. One day as I prepared for a test in reading the Koran, I decided that I wanted to chant it to my teacher instead of simply reading it. I made this decision because chanting or singing the Koran was considered to be more valuable than reading it. In preparation for this I practiced very hard each day and night. When the day finally arrived for me to chant the Koran for my teacher, I was certain that he would like it so much that he would give me a very good grade. However, his reaction was much different than I had expected it to be. I was shocked with disbelief when he announced that I failed the exams. He said that I chanted the Koran as if I was singing "pop music"!

I thought about how I had sung the Koran from my heart and now the teacher was telling me that this was not good enough. Because I had expressed myself from the depths of my heart, I was so deeply wounded by this that I became disappointed with my religion altogether. In fact, I determined that I did not want to have anything to do with any religion ever again!

Because my heart was broken when my teacher told me lies and cast doubt about the Resurrection of Jesus, my disappointments began to multiply. Like so many theologians today, he had attacked the very foundation of the Christian faith: the Resurrection of Jesus Christ.

Jesus Is Risen

There are many schools of thought about the Resurrection of Jesus. Some scholars and philosophers try to prove that Jesus was not resurrected. Some contend that Jesus had a twin brother, and that when Jesus died on the cross, His brother replaced Him.

Some scholars even deny the historical existence of Jesus Christ. They consider Jesus to be a myth. Here are some of the facts that prove that Jesus Christ was truly resurrected.

1. The Seal, which was on the tomb, was broken.

It is written in Matthew 27:66 that after the burial of Jesus in the tomb, a large stone was put in the front of the entrance, the tomb was sealed, and guards were posted to keep watch to ensure that no one could come near the tomb. The seal was the symbol of the authority and power of the Roman Empire. If someone broke the seal, he had broken the rules of the Roman Empire. His punishment would therefore have been a death sentence of an upside-down crucifixion. Thus, no one would even dare to go near the tomb and break the seal.

2. The large stone was moved.

It is written that the stone was rolled away by an angel. Historians tell us that these kinds of stones were normally huge, weighing an average of 1.5 to 2 tons (almost 2,000 kilograms). So how could one *person or a group of people push away this huge stone? When you read the Bible carefully, you will find out that the stone was rolled against the tomb's entrance.*

"Rolled against" means that the stone was so heavy that carrying it would have been impossible. Along with this, the tomb was set on a slope. Matthew 28:2 says that an angel "rolled back" the stone. This tells us that the angel pushed the stone upwards on the slope. Pushing the two-ton stone upwards cannot be done by a human being.

3. THE ROMAN GUARDS

The guards that surrounded the tomb were well trained. They knew that they would be killed if they did not obey the orders they had been given. How could someone possibly have gone unnoticed as they passed through these guards, opened the tomb and stole the body of Jesus?

4. THE EMPTY TOMB AND THE BURIAL CLOTH

We read that there was no one in the tomb, but the burial cloth remained intact. In other words, it was still in the same exact form as it had been when it was wrapped around Jesus' body. How could this have been possible if someone had indeed stolen the body of Jesus? How could someone have unwrapped the body of Jesus and brought Him out while the form of the linen cloth in the tomb remained the same?

Our Christian faith is based upon the Resurrection of Jesus Christ. The Resurrection of Jesus Christ is

8

what makes Christianity so unique and special. Out of the thousands of belief systems in the world, Christianity is the only one that provides historical evidence of resurrection. The apostle Paul says, "And if Christ has not been raised, our preaching is useless and so your faith" (1 Cor. 15:14). It was by believing in the Resurrection that the disciples received power to preach the gospel. Also, all the messages of the gospel are based on the fact that Jesus is alive. And because Jesus Christ is alive, He can do the same things today that He did during His three years of ministry while He was in bodily form here on earth. Today He is still healing the sick, forgiving sin, feeding the hungry and more.

Without the Resurrection, the passage in Hebrews 13:8 would never be valid: "Jesus Christ is the same yesterday, today and forever more." If the doubters of historical evidence are correct and Jesus is not resurrected, then we have no hope for healing, no hope for forgiveness, no hope for prosperity, no hope for our families and no hope for our nations.

THE COLD WEST

When my religion teacher stole from me my faith that Jesus had been resurrected, my inner world collapsed and my hope began to vanish into nothing but rebellion and anger.

My disillusionment led me to begin reading books I did not even understand. I was sixteen when I read Karl Marx and Lenin's books on Communism. I forgot about Jesus, the plastic cross and my friend. Instead, I joined a group of intellectual students in the high school. I was blacklisted many times from lessons on religion because I would ask silly questions, even denying the existence of God. Finally, I was expelled from the school altogether. But, thank God, that same week my family and I were set to leave the country and head to the West!

My parents sold everything we had—our house, our cars, our companies—everything.

"You must be brave and strong and study very well," my father told me. "Because of you, we are selling everything we have in order to go to the West."

My father told me that they were making a very big sacrifice for me and asked me to not disappoint them. I heard his words, but I had other things on my mind. My friends told me that girls in the West are tall, blond and beautiful. They also told me that I should have a girlfriend there because that would prove that I am a real man!

I suddenly entered a totally different world from what I had left in my country, with its old traditions where women were covered from head to foot. At the airport I saw two men kissing. I saw half-naked women walking around. I thought to myself, *Wow, if they did this in my country, these people would be stoned to death!*

Everything was new for me—the people, the language, the TV channels. I always thought I was tall, but when I saw the people in the West, I felt I was the shortest guy in the world. Although the West was new for me, I could sense that other people looked at me as though I was very different. In fact, I felt I was different. People would look at me as if I had come from the jungle, or like I was some kind of strange plant. I could also sense that some people did not like me.

SCHOOL IN THE WEST

The time soon came for me to attend a school to learn the new language. It was terrible, but I tried hard and did my very best. And guess what! I got a new friend, a born-again African boy. Even in the West, my first friend was a Christian!

We studied together day and night. Sometimes we would study until late at night just to prove that we foreigners are also intelligent. We learned the new language in less than six months, and after a year we were placed in A-level classes. This guaranteed us placement in any university we wanted to attend. Even local papers ran stories about us.

My African friend was humble and smart. The one and only topic we always fought about was Jesus Christ. My friend would always talk to me about Him, but I did not want to hear of it anymore. A lot had happened since my first friend had told me about Jesus. In fact, I even tried to influence this new friend with my ideas and tried to convince him to become an atheist. However, somehow he was stronger than I was! We argued and debated many times and always ended up fighting. I denied Jesus, ridiculed Him and even wrote against Him. I did these things because I was trying to hide something, and my African friend knew all about this. I was hiding my disappointments with God. I did not want to be disappointed again, so I allowed myself to believe that Jesus was nothing but a lie!

The more I rebelled, the more sad and depressed I became. I thought I could only become somebody through my studies, so I put all my efforts into studying hard. Because I did not associate with anyone, my friends used to call me "grandpa." While they spent their time drinking or hanging out with their girlfriends, I stayed home and did my homework until late into the night. Back then, I wanted to be an international lawyer who would fight for the rights of people in Third-World countries. In my own way, I wanted to be a hero of the poor and oppressed. For some reason, after high school I changed my mind and decided to study Third-World sociology.

I began to dream and develop my own ideas about how to change the world. But, one day, my favorite professor burst my bubble when he said, "It is simply not possible to change the world."

He said he had tried to do it for the last twenty-five years, and he had found out that it simply did not work! Disappointed and discouraged again, I entered a period of dark emptiness. I did not care about anything or anybody. All I cared about was myself and about my life. I became aggressive and harsh toward my family and friends.

Jesus Is the Answer!

In the middle of all this, I got to know a girl named Sarah, who lived a few houses away from us. Every morning I would see this beautiful Korean girl, with long hair, singing as she walked to the subway!

I fell in love with her and she also fell for me, but we didn't dare to tell each other about the burning love within us. When my family was about to move to a new neighborhood, she approached me. We then became friends and went out on a date. After she told me about her life, I realized how much she had suffered. A small part of her face was burned when she was a little girl; even today there is still a burn mark on her face. But she was so relaxed and beautiful that I did not even notice this mark of suffering.

I had noticed that most women in the West spent thousands of dollars for cosmetics to hide their imperfections, so it amazed me how my friend could handle hers without being depressed. The more I got to know her, the more her joy seemed to put a spotlight on the miserable life I led. So, I decided to ask her about her secret for being content and satisfied in life. What was it that was giving her so much power and inner peace? What was it that made her so special and joyful? I asked her if she was taking some kind of drug that gave her this happiness.

She was silent for a while, and then she said, "No, I am not using any drugs."

She took out a small book and said, "This is what I use."

She told me that she had wanted to give me this book for a long time but had been waiting for the right opportunity. I took the book and read its cover, *The Holy Bible.*

"How can a book make you happy and peaceful?" I asked her.

I told her that my library was filled with books, but none of them had ever made me happy. In fact, they actually made me more depressed!

"It is not the book alone that makes me happy, but the Person behind the book," she answered. She looked at me and said, "Jesus is the Answer!"

I would soon learn that many people, like myself, are looking for happiness and joy. Some are surrounded by possessions, money and position, and yet there is still a kind of poverty within them. Emptiness and misery rule their lives. Such lack, such vacuums of love can only be filled once that person has experienced the living God.

Once the immortal God touches the mortal man through Jesus Christ, that man or woman will have everlasting joy and happiness. Healing of both body and soul takes place. Even today, Jesus Christ wants to be the Lord of our lives. He wants to give the best to His people. All this starts with Jesus. I was about to learn that Jesus was the answer I had been searching for my whole life.

MY ANSWERS

In a moment of time, all of my memories of learning about Jesus flashed back when my girlfriend, who is my wife today, declared that Jesus is the answer. I remembered my friend, the plastic cross and the picture of Jesus. In my heart, I said, "Oh no, not again!"

I told her that my family was Muslim, and if I want to believe, I'll have to simply refocus again on my own religion that I had received at birth.

"I don't need any religion anyway," I told her. "Besides, if I become a Christian, I will be banned from my family, and I will lose my rights."

In reply, she said, "Jesus Christ is not a religion! Jesus Christ is not something that you get at birth; He is a choice you make once and forever."

She told me that there are many so-called Christians who think they became Christians at birth, but they have never had a personal experience with Christ. "Jesus is a living Person who wants to have a relationship with us every day," she said. "He wants to be our Friend for life."

I knew she was right. I had never made the choice to be a Muslim, a Jew or a Hindu. I was simply born into the religion of my parents. I understood that as an adult I had the right to choose.

She told me that Jesus Christ is not received at birth, but by our hearts; Jesus Christ is not received because of our culture, but because of our choice!

I did not like hearing what she had to say, so I told her, "I am an educated man that studies in one of the biggest universities in the world. I already have knowledge and intellect, so, therefore, I do not need God nor His Jesus to help me out."

I even went so far as to tell her, "I am the god of my

own life."

She simply said, "Even all the knowledge of the world cannot explain the surpassing power of God."

Of course, she was right. All I had to do was consider a small insect and how even the greatest scientists in the world cannot create an insect. Maybe they can make a model, but it still would not be the real thing. I had to come to terms with the fact that the entire world was created by an Intelligence that cannot be explained by man-made knowledge.

After many years now, I was beginning to come to grips with the fact that no one can fight God, and no one can imitate Him. A sinful man such as I could never compete with the holy God. To my astonishment, I was beginning to realize that all the knowledge in the world, in all the billions of books in thousands of libraries around the world, couldn't even come close to comparing with the power and the intelligence of the almighty God.

HATRED AND ANGER

Our conversation led me to be more confused and angry. I thought I had it all figured out, and now I was discovering that I was not my own god. Every time I visited her family, they would question me, and try to convince me to be born again. Nothing made me angrier. To make matters worse, my girlfriend, Sarah, attended church on Sundays. I did not agree with her on this because Sunday was my only free day. On Sundays, I wanted to have fun and go on dates with her, but she always refused to go with me. Instead, she would go to church and then tell me all about what the pastor had preached. One day I got so angry that I even thought about how I would like to burn down the church building. Deep in my heart, I knew my anger was wrong.

Early one morning, Sarah phoned to say that her mother wished to see me. When I arrived, her mother said, "Young man, if you want to marry my daughter, you must be born again. You must give your life totally to Jesus."

I grew furious during the four hours we discussed this. Finally, I told her, "Take your daughter. I no longer want her."

I stood up, flung open the door and left. After that, the pressure from her family caused my relationship with Sarah to become more difficult.

A NEW FRIEND

After many arguments, I broke down and decided to visit the church where Sarah went. It was a nice place; people there seemed to be happy, but somehow I found them to be too pushy.

The day I visited the church was special because they had a guest whose name was Philip. At that time, he was a Korean missionary who had come to stay in our country. Everyone was waiting for him to arrive that day. The Korean pastor picked him up at the airport. Philip, his wife, Grace, and their little boy, Daniel, eventually arrived. The moment I saw Philip, he struck me as a charismatic and sympathetic person.

We became friends. He did not ask me any questions about being born again. Instead, he was interested in me. He asked questions about my fatherland, my family and my studies. Several times he invited me to his house. We had a really great time listening to music and talking about life. But one day, I remember he asked me a serious and unexpected question.

"Are you saved?" he asked.

I was puzzled by this question. Because I had grown up with religion, somehow I believed in a heaven and a hell. I knew that there must be some sort of punishment for those who do evil and never get punished while on earth. Even so, I could not answer Philip.

I knew my life was filled with sin; therefore, I could not say I would go to heaven. I also could not say that I would go to hell because I did not want to go there. I knew I was a sinner, and so trying to answer his question confounded me.

WHERE ARE YOU GOING?

How about you? Are you saved? Where are you going? Are you sure where you will end up after death? Let me put it in a different way: Would you ride in a plane if you knew beforehand that it was going to crash? Of course not! By the same token, would you consciously live a life that will lead you to death and destruction, to hell and everlasting punishment? There is no assurance in this life. We do not know what will happen to us tomorrow or even five minutes from now.

For thousands of years the human race has been trying to prepare a place in Paradise and to ensure everlasting life. Some tried to do this through ceremonial practices, some by obeying the Law of Moses. During the Middle Ages, some tried to buy the key to heaven by donating huge amounts of money or large tracts of land to the Catholic Church. But none of these could give anyone the assurance of being saved.

> *Thanks be to God, He sent Jesus Christ, His Son, to save us and to set us free from bondage. Jesus Christ is the only way of salvation. He sacrificed His life for us so that we may live eternally with Him. Jesus Christ has paid the price for you. Live a life worthy of Him and of His name!*

I REJECTED MY FRIEND

Philip and I became good friends. I visited his home regularly. During one of my visits, we had a serious conversation about Jesus being God. I never could understand why Christians could worship three Gods; it was something new to me. I got so angry with Philip that I told him I never wanted to go to his house again. I had determined in my mind that I didn't want to hear these stupid philosophies ever again.

Tears filled his eyes and his voice shook as my friend told me that he respected my decision and he would never disturb me again.

I bid him goodbye and left his house determined to look after my own life and find the truth for myself. I completely avoided him for over a year. I even ignored him whenever I saw his car pass by me.

YOU WILL WORK FOR GOD

Even though I felt miserable about what I had done to Philip, my pride kept me from calling or going to see him. I was grieving inside, but my pride held me back.

At that time, I was working at the post office sorting letters and carrying heavy boxes to various departments. One night while I was working there, I met a new man. I asked his name, and we quickly became friends.

When I asked him if he had other jobs besides the one at the post office, he said, "I work for the Lord. I sing for Him."

I did not understand what he meant so I asked him, "Who is the Lord?"

He quickly replied, "Jesus Christ, of course."

I thought to myself, *What does this Jesus want from me? Everywhere I go, I hear His name!*

I told the man, "I am getting sick of His name."

The man looked straight at me and said, "You know what? One day you will be working for Jesus full-time. You will be a man of God."

I laughed and said, "I am not a Christian! How can it be possible for me to work for Jesus?"

But he said he knew it for sure! Early that morning when I came home, the man's voice kept echoing in my soul: "You will work for God…You will work for God…You will be a man of God."

The next night when I went back to work at the post office, I had planned to ask the man more questions; but I did not see him anywhere. I went to my supervisor and asked her if she knew of a man with that name who had worked in the office the night before.

She told me that she did not know a man by that name! Looking back, I wonder who that man could have been. An angel? A prophet? Or just an ordinary Christian?

GOD HAS A PLAN FOR YOU

Today, after many years, I now fully understand that what the man said was true. I am now working for the Lord and preaching the gospel. At that time I rebelled against it. I was not yet a Christian, so I could not see that one day, I would be working for Someone I did not believe in at that time.

But despite my rebellion and lack of understanding at that time, God did indeed have a plan for me. He was working on me, preparing me quietly for the outworking of His plan and purpose for my life.

God also has a plan for you. You were born for a purpose; you were not born accidentally. Before you were born, God called you by name. His plan for you is perfect as long as you choose to live according to His plan. There is so much to know about God; there is so much to receive from God. In His time, He will reveal more to you. If you are a born-again Christian, I challenge you with this thought: There is much more in store for you than you could ever think or imagine.

There is more to it than going to church on Sunday morning, more to it than singing in the choir. There is more to it than praying in tongues and feeling high in the Spirit. Please do not limit the Holy Spirit. Let His perfect plan be manifested in your life and expect the great things that God has promised to you!

MY DREAM

One night I had a mysterious dream. I was dressed in a beautiful suit, wearing a nice necktie and carrying a Samsonite bag as I walked down the streets of Jerusalem. I was on my way to a business meeting, but an old man sitting beside a lake caught my attention. He had a long white hair and a long gray beard. He was sitting at a big wooden office table that was filled with many old books. The water looked very inviting and a little voice in my heart told me to throw myself into the water. Suddenly, I jumped into the water in my beautiful suit, holding my expensive bag. The fresh water felt so good, and it made me feel relieved. Then, my feet touched something. I picked it up and saw that it was a cup! I turned the cup and saw that there was a Hebrew word on the bottom of the cup. I did not understand the word, so I went to the old man to show him the cup.

The old man jumped out of his chair, and kissed and hugged me. He said he had been looking for this cup all his life. He said his hair had grown white because of his search, and yet he could not find it. He was surprised that I had jumped in the water near his study table and so easily found what he had been looking throughout his whole life.

"What is it that is so important about this cup?" I asked.

He said, "This cup belonged to John the Baptist during the time of Jesus. He probably used it for baptism."

I was so shocked that I woke up from my sleep. I felt unsettled about this and so I said to myself, *It was just a dream!* I did not know what the dream meant then, but now I know its meaning. I had found the cup of John the Baptist. He was the one who prepared the way of the Lord Jesus Christ. He preached about Jesus Christ and His coming and called people to repent and be baptized.

Similarly, God was preparing me to one day be a preacher of the gospel of Jesus Christ, just like other Spirit-filled preachers and men of God. God was telling me through the dream that one day I would be calling people to repentance, and preaching to the world about the coming of Jesus Christ. Because of this call on my life, I needed to get into that water, which is a symbol of the Holy Spirit. In order to find that cup or step into the call God had on my life, I had to throw myself into the water.

Get in the Water

God says in Zechariah 4:6, "Not by might nor by power, but my Spirit, saith the Lord of hosts" (KJV).

Water is a symbol of the Holy Spirit. Sadly, many people ignore the Holy Spirit, the third Person of the Godhead. However, Jesus Christ Himself promised His disciples that one day they would be filled with the Holy Spirit. He instructed them not to leave Jerusalem, but to wait until they had received the Holy Spirit, "You will receive power after the Holy Spirit is come upon you" (Acts 1:7, KJV). Only then would they be ready to go to Judea, to Samaria and to the end of the world.

The early church was not a man-made organization or a denomination. At that time, church leaders did not go through a five-year theological school program. Of course, the church then also did not have telephones, fax machines or Internet access with which to reach the world. They only had one thing that turned the Roman Empire upside down—the power of the Holy Spirit.

Many people today are so stuck in their own rules and regulations that they forget the Spirit of God. You can try everything on your own and yet not be successful. Even if you have the most beautiful church building on earth, God cannot use you if you are not on fire with the Holy Spirit and be obedient to His voice.

God is not interested in the shape of our religiosity or the manners of our worship, He is interested in the depth of our relationship with Him.

We must be Spirit-filled when we are doing His work. How loud we pray in tongues or how hard we shake under the power of the Holy Spirit is not a good measurement of the quality of our walk with God. Instead, a Spirit-filled worker who is pleasing to God will be someone who is ready to risk everything and do what the Spirit asks him to do!

Remember the old man beside the lake? His hair had grown white; he looked like one of those clever professors. All of his life he had been looking for the thing which I had found in the dream in less than five minutes. The only difference between that old man and me was that I jumped in the water, and he did not!

He was sitting behind his glorious study table surrounded by books, but he was not able to find the cup. He stood outside looking for something that was inside. Like the old man, many people today are standing outside the "water."

Many people, even some who go to church, long

to be used by God, but they are looking for the truth by their own strength.

However, to discover the truth they must be filled by God's Spirit. They must give the Spirit of God freedom to move in their hearts, lives, ministries and churches. By personal experience, I know that this works, so much so that in less than three years my ministry reached more than eighty nations of the world. I will explain more about this later in this book.

As you read this book, listen to the Holy Spirit's voice. He wants to be your Friend and Guide in everything you do. He is ready for you. If you hear Him and obey Him, many doors will be opened to you.

Because I seemed to have so many early experiences with Christians, I wondered why I must always be the target of Christians. My boyhood friend who gave me the plastic cross, the man I met when I worked at my post office, my friend Philip whom I rejected and my dream, all of these experiences kept me wondering; but I still continued fighting and arguing with Christian friends.

Chapter 2

Someone Is Knocking at the Door

TIME PASSED BY. WHILE STUDYING AT THE UNIVERSITY, I was also running a business with a friend. Life was going well, so I decided to marry Sarah. We were quite excited and challenged by the wedding preparations. Sarah's mother kept saying I needed to be born again. The more she nagged, the more stubborn I became. After all the arrangements and hard work had been made by my family and Sarah's, the sacred day of the wedding came at last!

My future mother-in-law told me that if I did not want to become a Christian, then out of respect for her I should at least marry in a church. Even though I was uncomfortable with the idea, I agreed to marry in the Korean Church anyway. I was so nervous on my wedding day that I did not even know how to put on my shoes. I was in a panic. I wondered how my family could sit in church—and a Korean-speaking church at that!

Sarah was so beautiful that day that she looked like an angel to me. The church was filled with Koreans and people from the Middle East. Two totally different cultures met in church on our wedding day.

Everyone sat down as the pianist started to play. Everyone waited for Sarah to walk down the aisle. She came in with her uncle. He placed her hand in my hand. Now Sarah and I were standing before the preacher. I expected him to simply ask me a few questions and I would say yes, then Sarah would also answer yes to his questions, and it would quickly be over and he would declare us man and wife. But no, it didn't go that way at all. Instead, the man started to preach in Korean, and his sermon lasted for more than forty minutes. There I was, standing while my family and I heard nothing but "ching chung chung . . . " Tired and angry, I wanted to hit the preacher and tell him, "Just ask the questions and marry us!" Thank God, I didn't do it!

Finally, the preacher asked the questions we had long been waiting for. I said yes even before he finished his questions. At last, we were married! Hallelujah! We were now headed toward a new life and a new beginning together.

SOMEONE BEHIND THE DOOR!

I was more excited about our honeymoon than the wedding ceremony. The day after we were married, we traveled to Costa Brava, a wonderful tourist area in Spain. I liked the sea, so we swam every day. At night we went to a restaurant or café to eat and drink. Sarah had stopped talking about Jesus Christ for some time, so we talked about other things and our future plans. We planned to start a new business and look for a new house. We talked until dark.

One night while we were still on our honeymoon, we ate in a restaurant, and with our new dreams we went back to our hotel to rest and sleep. Sarah fell asleep the minute she laid her head on the pillow, but I couldn't sleep. It was already three in the morning; it was dark outside, and I could hear some faint disco music.

While laying in bed thinking about the future, I heard this extraordinary man's voice in our room. The voice called my name and said, "Here I am, I stand behind the door of your heart and I knock. If you open the door, I will come in and live with you."

I thought I was dreaming, but I was awake! I pinched myself and looked at my watch. Was there someone in our room? The voice repeated again, "Here I am, I stand behind the door of your heart and I knock. If you open the door, I will come in and live and drink with you." I had never heard such a beautiful and powerful voice before! I knew that what was happening was real. I said to the voice, "Sir! Before you enter, tell me who you are!"

The voice said, "My son! Don't you know Me? I am your Lord King Jesus Christ, the one you have persecuted for so long!"

While He was saying this, I was filled with Holy Spirit! I heard the sound of thousands of angels singing and rejoicing in the Lord. Then the Lord spoke to me in an unknown language, but amazingly, I could understand what He was saying. He said I must go back to my city where He would use me to preach the gospel to many people. He said that I must tell the world that He is alive and is coming soon! That night I was born again. I had a new life and a new beginning. I realized that I was a sinner and no one would be able to forgive my sins: no tradition, no rules of religion, no law and no animal sacrifice. Only Jesus Christ dying on the cross could pay the price for my sins. I realized that the wages of sin is the death of ending up in eternal punishment.

I realized that Someone had died for me; Someone suffered in my place. His blood paid the price on the cross at Calvary. He became the Lamb of God that took away my sins. "Someone died for me . . . Someone died for me . . . " is still echoing in my ears, even today!

SOMEONE IS CALLING YOU

Jesus Christ said, "Behold, I stand at the door and knock. If anyone hears My voice and opens the door. I will come in to him and dine with him, and he with Me" (Rev. 3:20, NKJV).

Today Jesus is still knocking at the door of our lives. We must open the door and let Him come in and be our Master and King. Jesus is knocking at the doors of our hearts, our families, our homes, our society and our governments. Once we open these doors for Jesus Christ and His gospel, our lives and our world will drastically change.

You and I may have experienced a new birth twenty years ago, but that is not today! Our God is the God of today. He dwells in the "Now." He is Emmanuel, "God with us," and He wants to be our Lord today. Opening the door of hearts means being obedient to His voice and following what He says to us. It is easy to be called a Christian, but it is difficult to be called a disciple!

Billions of people in the world today are called Christians, but Jesus Christ is looking for disciples. He is looking for men and women who will accept

His call, who will swim against the currents of this world, who will say no to the things the world will try to sell to them and who will say yes to God and His voice.

And if you are not a disciple yet, consider this: The same Jesus Christ who called me into His kingdom is saying the same words to you! Whoever you are, He stands behind the door, gently waiting for you to open the door.

What is behind the door? Is there grief? Is there sadness? Is there sickness? Is there anger? I tell you the truth, when Jesus Christ enters the room of your heart, all these things will be changed and healed, some gradually and some immediately. The coming of Jesus Christ in my life changed me. I became a softer person, I was no longer hot-tempered like I had been before. Are you ready today to open your heart?

New Birth

I remember my first morning in the Lord. Sarah was utterly shocked when I announced to her, "I am a Christian!" She was shocked, but also full of joy. She said that after two years God had finally answered her prayers. The honeymoon was so beautiful, and while I was walking down the busy streets of Costa Brava, I wanted to talk to everyone about Jesus. I was singing the whole day long! I felt fresh, so new!

I then understood what my Christian friends had meant when they told me about being born again. I thought about the plastic cross and my school friend. I now hoped

I could find him and tell him that I no longer needed a plastic cross, because the real Cross was now within me, inside me. And this was the Cross no one could take away.

> *Christians commonly use the terms "new birth" or "born again" today. In fact, we have used them loosely; and, in many cases, we have forgotten their real meanings. In some countries like the Philippines, the majority of traditional Christians consider the born-again Christians to be a sect. They have no idea about the real meaning of the term.*
>
> *The person who used the term born again for the first time was Jesus Christ Himself. You may know the story from the Gospel of John, chapter three. Nicodemus, a Pharisee or a teacher of the law went to Jesus by night to ask Him questions. In response to Nicodemus' questions, Jesus Christ said something very amazing: "I tell you the truth, no one can see the kingdom of God unless he is born again" (John 3:3).*
>
> *Jesus went on to say, "I tell you the truth, no one can see the kingdom of God unless he is born of water and spirit. Flesh gives birth to flesh and Spirit gives birth to spirit" (John 3:5–6).*
>
> *Please notice that Jesus never said you have to be a Catholic, Methodist, Pentecostal or Southern Baptist to enter the kingdom of God. No! He simply said you need to be born again. Being born again means you have decided with all your heart and mind to follow Jesus Christ and have yielded your heart to His Holy Spirit.*
>
> *Being born again starts with our decision to*

follow Christ and there is no turning back. Once we have made that decision we need to be baptized in water. Jesus said, "He who believes and is baptized, will be saved" (Mark 16:16, NKJV).

He also commanded His disciples to go to all the nations and preach the gospel and to baptize them in the name of the Father, Son and the Holy Spirit. Baptism in water is a sign of obedience to God's voice. But baptism is also a choice; it is not a decision from someone else. Some say they were baptized when they were babies. But they themselves did not make that decision! Baptism is a form of repentance, an action of dying with Jesus and being buried with Him. When we rise up from the water, we are new and fresh, heading for a new life. Jesus said something more about being born again, namely being born of the Spirit.

John the Baptist told people of being baptized in fire. He said, "I baptize you with water for repentance. But after me will come one who is more powerful than I, whose sandals I am not fit to carry. He will baptize you with the Holy Spirit and with fire" (Matt. 3:11).

Jesus commanded His disciples to be filled with the Holy Spirit. He urged them not to leave Jerusalem but to wait until the Holy Spirit had come upon them, and then they would be witnesses to all the nations. (See Acts 2.)

On the day of Pentecost, the Holy Spirit came upon the disciples. They were filled with the Holy Spirit and began to speak in other languages. They received power and were changed. The same Peter *who denied Jesus three times now became bold in witnessing for Christ. The doubting Thomas was changed into a powerful witness.* The church of Jesus Christ was on fire! *The same thing happened with Saul, a persecutor of Christians. On the way to Damascus, he had a personal encounter with Jesus Christ. He then was changed into a disciple and an apostle of Christ to the nations of the world.*

Many people are confused about being born again. They limit this event by thinking that being born again means only praying in tongues or having other gifts of the Holy Spirit. Please understand that being born again is not just having a new language or a gift. Being born again is also not only about calling out to Jesus, "Lord, Lord."

Being born again means having a new way of life that is worthy of Christ. Some people do pray in tongues, but their attitudes are similar to the devil's people! Some claim they are born again, but they treat their husbands or wives worse than worldly people do. This is not about what we call ourselves, and it is not about what we claim to be. It is about living a life in God's holiness, living a life by the Spirit of God and His love.

Love is the greatest sign of being born again. I am not talking about worldly love. I am talking about Christ-like love! Paul said in 1 Corinthians 13:1–2, "If I speak in tongues of men or angels, but have not love, I am only a resounding gong or a clanging cymbal. If I have the gift of prophecy and can fathom all the mysteries and all knowledge, and if I have faith that can move mountains, but have not love, I am nothing."

In other words, Paul says that even if we have all of the gifts, we are nothing if we do not practice the love of Christ. Of course, if we are nothing, we cannot also be born again! Being born again means total surrender to Jesus Christ and His Holy Spirit.

BE SURE YOU ARE SAVED!

Once we are really born again, the Holy Spirit will enter into our lives. He will guide us daily and show us our path in Christ. He will protect us from sin and from our past hurts. Giving the Holy Spirit the freedom to control our lives will keep us from falling. The Holy Spirit assures us that we are saved, not by religious practices or by Bible knowledge, but because of God's favor and grace. The Bible says that we are saved by grace and not by our deeds. (See Ephesians 2:8–9.)

Many people today are not sure of their salvation. Some of them have even grown up in the church, and yet they are not sure where they would end up if they died today. If you yourself are not sure about this, if you doubt your salvation today, then you need to be born again—not only by name—but also by heart.

I tell you the truth: Right now this book is being used by the Holy Spirit to bring you back to God. God is present while you are reading these very words. Just pray in your heart and ask the Lord to come into your life. Tell Him that you want to be made new, that you want to receive the fresh anointing from the Holy Spirit. Confess to Him that you love Him, you know He died for you and you know that His shed blood forgives your sins. Ask the Holy Spirit to lead you and to be your Friend for the rest of your life. Try Him!

Now that you have done this, you can be 100 percent sure that you are saved. However, the goal of this book is not to simply bring you to the point of salvation and then leave you there. As you continue reading this book, you will pass beyond the level of just being satisfied with your salvation. You will move forward into the place where you will also produce lasting fruit.

GRADUAL PROCESS

Some people think their characters will immediately change when they are born again. This is only partly true because God changes some things immediately, while others are changed gradually.

My own testimony is an example of this. I had a lot of weaknesses, one of them was being hot-tempered. My hot temper did not change overnight. Instead, as the Holy Spirit controlled my life, He slowly changed me into a softer person.

If all of God's miracles in our lives came all at once, we might not be able to handle all of the changes at once.

We must realize that although we are born again, we are still humans. This means that we can, and will, make mistakes. However, when we rely on God's grace, He will help us to stand back up on our feet again. Over time we will become more and more stable in the Lord, but life's challenges will always cause us to rely on Him rather than on our own strength.

The Bible story of Esther is a good picture of how God changes us gradually. It is one of my favorite passages of scripture. Before becoming the queen of Persia, she received beauty treatments of perfumes and oils for a whole year. After she was washed with all of these treatments of oil and perfume, she became the queen!

This is similar to the beauty treatments we receive from Jesus when we accept Him as our Lord and Savior. Until we are fully in God's presence in heaven, He will give us a daily beauty treatment through His Holy Spirit. Just as Esther was purified by bathing in the oil, He will purify us through the Holy Spirit until the last moment of our physical life here on earth. Oil is the symbol of the Holy Spirit. He will anoint you with His oil, and your life will be changed just like Esther's life was changed. Everyone who believes in Him will become a new creation, born again into a new life. Before you appear before God's throne, He will change you from glory to glory.

PROBLEM FREE?

Many people think that by being born again and having Jesus enter their lives, they will be problem-free. However, this is simply not the case. We will face difficulties and challenges even though God is *able to solve any problem and absolutely nothing is too difficult for Him. As long as we are living on this side of eternity, there will be still problems and challenges coming on our road, but God will use them to build us up and make us stronger. Yes, there will always be problems, but now you will no longer be fighting alone. There is Somebody with you! His name is the Holy Spirit.*

Chapter 3

"I Have a Present for You"

MY HONEYMOON WAS NOT ONLY A HONEYMOON with my wife, but also a honeymoon with Jesus Christ. Looking back after so many years, it seems that every day since then, I have done nothing except love Jesus Christ: "Eating *with* Him, drinking *with* Him," and taking up my cross and following Him.

ADVENTURES STARTED

In the beginning of my new life, I thought it was the end because I was now born again. Because I felt happy, I thought I could still continue doing my job as a businessman and as a university student. But in my heart of hearts, I knew I was really lying to myself. Deep in my heart, I knew this was not the end, but instead it was the beginning of new adventures with the Lord. Deep in my heart, I desired to share with everybody about Christ. I had the "Light of the world" inside me, and I could not keep Him in the little room of my own heart. I knew He wanted to use me. I was in love with Jesus, and I wanted to share this love with my family, friends and other people.

Another one of the greatest signs of being born again is having a passion and love for sharing what Jesus Christ has done for you. Never lose this passion and power in your life.

Some Christians, as they grow older in the Lord, lose their passion for sharing the simplicity of Jesus' gospel. They become so wrapped up in theologies or man-made teachings that they forget the basics of sharing the Good News with the unsaved around them. Although this passion for sharing the gospel may bring us a lot of persecution from people around us, we must not lose our joy and love for sharing Christ.

I HAVE A PRESENT FOR YOU

As soon as I came back from Spain, I remembered my friend, Joseph, who was also from the Middle East. He was raised in a quite liberal Muslim family. I knew him back in high school. He was an artist who came from an artistic family. Every time we had been together in the past we had always talked about art, religion and philosophy. Now that I was born again, I had made up my mind to share Jesus Christ with Joseph. I was certain that he would be touched and changed because I knew that Joseph had also been looking for truth in his life.

A few days after my arrival, I phoned him and invited him to come to my house for dinner. I told him I had a present for him and he should come and get it himself. So Joseph came to my home, and we ate and had fun. The whole evening I did not mention anything about my experience. We just talked about other things like holiday memories and looking at our honeymoon pictures.

Then Joseph asked me, "By the way, where is the present from Spain?" He also thanked me for thinking about him while I was in my honeymoon. I looked at him and said, "The thing I brought with me is something you cannot see with your eyes. It's invisible."

"But what is it?" he asked.

I looked straight at him and said, "It's Jesus Christ!"

For a moment there was silence; Joseph was puzzled. He then broke the silence and said, "Have you become a Christian?"

I said, "Yes, and I want you to become one." As I shared my experience, he remained quiet and listened. I told him that my present is the greatest present a person can get in life. My present for him is called salvation through Christ Jesus. I told him that the greatest present we can ever receive, the greatest miracle we can ever experience, is the salvation for our souls.

Joseph did not know what to say. He said that he needed time to think about it. When the evening came to an end and we said goodbye, Joseph went back home empty-handed, without any present from Spain that could be seen with the human eye. Instead, he left with a much greater gift than money could ever buy. He left my home with a heart filled with the knowledge of Jesus Christ. Just one week later he called me and said, "Sam, I want to receive Jesus in my life." I had this joy in my heart that no one could ever take away. I shared my gift of salvation with my friend, and he gave his life to Christ.

Not only was I overjoyed because my friend had received Jesus Christ, but now I had a new Christian companion. For Joseph and me, this was the beginning of a long journey together. He is still with me today. We travel together all over the world, and God is using him as a mighty Christian singer. I am proud of him and thankful to God for the privilege of laying my hand upon him.

POWER IN PRAYER

I also called Philip, the pastor whom I had rejected earlier. He was so overjoyed when I shared my testimony with him that he did not know what to say. All he could say was, "Hallelujah! Glory to God! I have been praying for your conversion for a long time."

God had answered his prayers, but he was not the only person who had been praying for me. I found out that a network of born-again Christians had been praying for my salvation for a long time. This shows that God answers prayers. If you are praying for someone, do not be weary and grow tired. Do not give up, for God is a faithful God. He knows when to answer your prayers. There is no prayer that God will keep unanswered and unheard. He hears even the most secret prayers you have hidden deep in your heart. Never forget that there is power in the prayers of the saints. Prayer is the motor of our hope in Jesus Christ.

WHAT IS PRAYER?

Prayer means talking or speaking with God in the same way that you would speak or talk to a person. God is our Father, so we can pray to Him in the way that we talk to our parents. Imagine yourself when you were still a child. When you wanted candy from your mother, you never said, "Oh, mother, who is the wife of my father, who cooks every day, who washes our dishes, heavenly greetings to you, can I please have a candy?" No, you would never ask your mother for candy in that way. Instead, you would ask her in the normal way: "Mom, I want a piece of candy." And then if she refused you, you would still continue to ask and cry until you received it. The same is true when we pray to God our Father. Just as Jesus used the word "Abba," which means "Daddy," we can be free to talk with our Father in a pleasant way.

The Hebrew words for prayer are sha'al, *which means "suggestions," and* proseuchomai, *which means "request from God." These words indicate that you can suggest to God your ideas and request from Him whatever you wish, even the small things. Do not think that God will laugh at you because of your small wishes.*

What can prayer do for you? According to James 5:13, prayer makes you free from your troubles. Are you in trouble? You should pray. Are you happy? Then sing songs of praise. Is any among you sick? Then he should call the elders of the church to pray over him and anoint him with oil in the name of the

Lord. The prayer offered in faith will make the sick person well; the Lord will raise him up. If he has sinned, he will be forgiven. (See James 5:13–15.)

So prayer makes you free from things like stress, marriage problems and bad habits. Through prayer you can also avoid temptations. In Matthew 26:41, Jesus said, "Watch and pray so that you will not fall into temptation. The spirit is willing, but the body is weak." In our daily lives we are surrounded by unbelievers, and by sins and temptations to sin. So if we want to be strong against the temptations of the world, we must pray every day.

The body of Christ needs to pray more than ever before because it is by prayer that we can influence families, cities and nations. Prayer can break down strongholds in every situation. Prayer can influence the history of a nation, break down curses and prepare nations for the kingdom.

Prayer can destroy the power of drugs and alcohol and bring a lost son back home, and bring peace and joy back into homes and lives!

There is power in prayer.

I WAS TRAINED

After I found out that so many people had prayed for me, I asked Philip to train me. I was serious about it, and I started from the basics. Philip had a one-year training plan, and every week I learned from him. As he explained things, they seemed so natural to me. Before, I could not understand the language of the born-again people, but now something had been changed inside me. Through the Holy Spirit, I could now understand everything Philip was teaching me. Doubt was no longer clouding my mind. I shared with others all that I learned from him. Those teachings were the foundation of my training and discipleship in the Lord. Even today, I look back to those teachings and apply them again and again in my life.

Foundational training is very essential for a baby Christian. Unfortunately, a lot of newly born-again Christians fall back into the world again because they lack foundational, systematic Bible training. Once the solid foundation has been laid in a person's life, there is less chance for that person to fall back.

I always say that we have the privilege of being able to use or hold a Bible in our hands, especially in the West. In some countries the Bible is not allowed and church fellowship is not permitted, and yet, in spite of these adversities, people love God and secretly try to get Bibles. Do you know why? It is because the Bible is the Word of God; the Bible is our written guide. The Bible is the voice of the Holy Spirit written down.

The Bible is the foundation of God's plans and teaching for our lives. There are many types of training today. I am not talking about theological training; I am talking about Spirit-filled basic training that will open many doors for us in our path of faith.

TIME TO SAY GOODBYE

During my one-year intensive training with Philip, I not only learned a lot, but I also enjoyed fellowship with him and his family. I remember Philip's wife preparing delicious food for us so that after the Bible training we could eat and be strengthened.

Philip had already told me that after I had completed my training with him, he would be going to Latvia to live and serve as a missionary. Because I did not think he was serious about it, I forgot about his plan. However, exactly one year after my training began, Philip called me to his house. He said, "Samuel, my job is finished. I was sent by God here to train you for a ministry that is waiting for you. Now I am going away so that you can grow." Then he looked at me straight in my eyes and said, "Joseph is your responsibility. You brought him to Christ, and you must teach and train him." He further said, "If Joseph falls, you are responsible." He was commissioning me to teach and train Joseph in the same way that he had taught and trained me.

I was shocked. In fact, his words terrified me a bit. This was hard for me to accept at the time, but now I understand that the God we serve is a God of purpose and planning. He had even sent someone from the other side of the world to train me. But when Philip's task was finished, the Lord sent him somewhere else.

SPIRITUAL ABORTION

Even after all of these years, Pastor Philip remains my dear friend and partner in the ministry. Even though he encouraged me to move on and continue to want more from God, it felt to me like he was going off and I was

44

being left alone again among the wolves.

I am convinced that if Philip had not encouraged, cared for and trained me during those early days of my foundational formation, I would have never become the person that I am today! I would probably have been a dead Christian in a dead church, disappointed with people and stressed out. But no, Philip did not abort my spiritual growth. He did not kill my leadership potentials. Instead, he nourished me through the wisdom of the Holy Spirit and God's voice.

Many people today are killing their children's spiritual potential before they are even formed. They abort their child's spiritual development by hanging on to their own old-fashioned, conservative ways of thinking. Also, many leaders spiritually 'kill' the future leaders, the world-changers of tomorrow, because they want to hang on to their old-fashioned doctrinal statements and rules and regulations.

But let us not abort these future hopes of Christ for the world. Let us raise disciples in the way God has planned them to become, not in way that we have planned them to be or do. Let us produce world-changers, difference-makers. The key to this is to encourage each other in the Lord.

Encouraging one another through the Holy Spirit is the engine of success and great achievements. I learned this from Philip, and today I do the same things to others whom I believe will be the world-changers of tomorrow in Christ.

Chapter 4

"I Will Obey"

P HILIP LEFT ME BEHIND WITH HIS TEACHINGS ABOUT JESUS Christ and Christianity. He left for Riga to start a Russian-speaking ministry. His words were still in my mind, "Joseph is your responsibility. I will go away so that you can start."

I Started

So there I was with a person whom I had brought to Christ: Joseph. He was the only person I had been commissioned to lead and teach everything I had learned from Philip. Left alone, I felt like a person who had just learned the basics of swimming in a pool, and now I had to swim on my own in the sea!

I was really nervous. I called Joseph and told him, "Please come to my Bible studies on Tuesday of next week. I want to teach you what I have learned from Philip. On Sundays we will go to church together." He agreed to my proposal.

Now I had one week to prepare the Bible studies. But while I was preparing the studies, God sent Someone to assist me!

I MET SOMEBODY

I needed help preparing the teachings for Joseph, but Philip was not there to answer my questions! I did not yet have his phone number to contact him. While I was wondering what to do, I suddenly could sense that there was Someone who could help me: *the Holy Spirit.*

After Philip left, I received a Friend that is much more powerful than him. He was, and still is, with me twenty-four hours a day. I needed help preparing the Bible studies, but I did not know how. Then the Holy Spirit whispered in my heart and said, "I will teach you. Allow Me, and I will guide you."

I knelt on my knees and asked the Holy Spirit to help me. From that day forward until today, every time I write a teaching I ask the Spirit of God to help me and guide me. I even printed a poster with the text: "Teach me, oh Holy Spirit." Before I even started to write one word of a teaching, I would always look at that poster. The Holy Spirit always was, and still is, my inspiration.

Jesus said the same to His disciples. He said that after He left, they should wait until they meet the Holy Spirit and are filled with Him. I thought I was alone. I thought I was dependent on a human being. But no, this was not the case at all. I was not alone. Jesus Christ died for me and is now seated at the right hand of God. He has sent the Holy Spirit to be our Guide and our Helper.

As I started the new challenge of leading Bible studies for one person, the Holy Spirit was with me in every moment and in every step of my preparations. But who is this Holy Spirit and what can He do for us? Before answering this question, I would like to clarify something about the Trinity.

TRINITY

Many people are confused about this word. They say, "How can God be three? God is only one."

The truth of the matter is that, God is One, but in Trinity! Let me explain it to you. According to Genesis, God created us in His own image. Since we are made in the image of God, every human being consists of a soul, spirit and body. These three make a human what he is.

I am not saying that while your body might be holding this book in Asia, your soul is somewhere in the USA, while your spirit is drinking a cup of tea in Europe. No, that would be ridiculous! Imagine that you have a body, but no soul; or you have a body, but no spirit. No, all these three are inseparable; they all make you the person you are.

God's triune nature is also referred to as the Godhead. I always like to use the term "Three-Unity." Indeed, Jesus Christ is the physical form of the Father and the Holy Spirit is the spiritual form of the Father and Jesus. They are all One. God is God in the inseparable unity between the Father, the Son and the Holy Spirit.

WHO IS THE HOLY SPIRIT?

Many have a wrong idea about the Holy Spirit. In the New Age movement, people think that they can access the Holy Spirit and communicate with Him even without being born again and without believing in Christ. I have seen a lot of people who say they have the Holy Spirit, and that He tells them things to do which are not even based upon God's Word. When I ask them if they have made the commitment to Christ, they say no. They say that all religions are the same. Despite their false statements, these people have never known the Holy Spirit! It would be impossible for them to have known the Holy Spirit because the Holy Spirit is only given to those who are committed disciples of Jesus Christ.

The first thing we must know about the Holy Spirit is that He will never come into our life as Friend if we do not receive Jesus Christ as our Lord and Savior. This is because they are inseparable! First Jesus, then the Holy Spirit will come.

The same is true concerning believing in Jesus Christ. You can never know Jesus if you do not know God the Father. You cannot deny God the Father but accept only Christ or the Holy Spirit. This is because they are all inseparable.

The second thing we need to know is that the Holy Spirit is not a manifestation, but a Giver of the manifestation. The Holy Spirit is not a tongue, but a Person. The Holy Spirit is not a prophecy, but a Person.

Many of us limit the Holy Spirit in these gifts that the Bible has promised us, but the Holy Spirit is more than these gifts. To understand this more clearly, imagine you are married to a person from Britain. Of course, your wife has a name and you would not say things like, "Hey, British woman, come here!" No, you would call her by her name. By the same token, you would not ignore her and only speak to her when you want her to cook something for you. You also would not say, "Hey, Cook, make some food for me." I think she would be quite offended and hurt by that comment.

However, nowadays we are doing the same with the Holy Spirit. We limit our view of Him to only certain spiritual things like speaking in tongues. I have seen people who think that He will be with them only when they pray in tongues. No, this is not true! The Holy Spirit is not bound by motion, time or space. He is a Person who is with us twenty-four hours a day—side by side when we walk, when we talk at home or at the work place. He touches us in every aspect of our daily lives, if we allow Him to do so!

The third thing we must know is that He is our Helper. In John 14, Jesus promises to give us the Holy Spirit, the Spirit of all truth, the Helper. We must realize that Holy Spirit is sent to us to support us and to guide us. The Holy Spirit will never do anything that we do not want or allow Him to do.

When I was not yet mature in my relationship with Holy Spirit, I thought that I must do "whatsoever people told me to do 'in the name of the Holy Spirit.'" I did not want people to be angry with me and leave me. I had a lot of people around me who said, "The Holy Spirit told me what you must do." Of course, some of the things they told me were from the Holy Spirit, but some were man-made ideas. We must be careful to pray for ourselves about the things people tell they have heard from the Holy Spirit for us, because our ultimate responsibility is to God and not to man. We must be pleasers of God, and not of men.

I was unsure of myself because I feared the Holy Spirit in a negative way. Maybe today, you also fear Him the same way I feared Him. I was not comfortable making decisions that I thought would possibly anger or disappoint the Holy Spirit because I had an unhealthy and unbalanced view of Him. I had to learn something that none of us must ever forget: The Holy Spirit is our Helper, and not vice versa. We are not helpers of the Holy Spirit. He does not need our help. We need His help! So let us not have fear in our fellowship with the Holy Spirit. We can see the importance of this in 1 John 4:18 when the apostle John says, "There is no fear in love. But perfect love drives out fear, because fear has to do with punishment. The one who fears is not made perfect in love."

Once I had an extraordinary experience that changed my life. I was invited to preach in the Philippines. Unusual things would happen when this one particular sister, a disciple in Christ, would begin to worship the Lord. She would go to people to browbeat them; her voice would change in a threatening way; and she always spoke strange things. In the beginning I thought it was the Holy Spirit, but later on I found out that it was not!

I would get so fearful every time she had those experiences. Whenever she did those things, I would ask myself, What have I done wrong this time that He is here? *I just let these things pass because they mostly occurred in small prayer groups.*

During the first day of the crusade, many people came there to hear God's message. When I started to preach, this sister stood up, shouted and disturbed the whole meeting. Some people could not stand the way that little sister looked, so they left. I still did not do anything to her, but continued to preach. That night in the hotel room, the Holy Spirit came on me and said, "Son, I did not send you 10,000 kilometers away to come to the Philippines to preach 'nothing.' If I had wanted to use that sister, I would have used her, and then you would not have needed to come here." *He further said,* "I am here to help you. I will do what you ask and wish." *Then I asked the Holy Spirit to help me understand Him better.*

He answered, "Consider this from today: We are partners. I will not do something you do not like! We are one." *The next day, strong in my heart, I called the girl to my hotel and told her everything. Her reactions changed suddenly. She started to beat herself and shout, saying that I had forsaken God.*

In response to this, I turned my face to the window and began to pray in my native language. I then addressed the demon spirit in the girl and asked certain questions in my language. However,

53

the demon in that girl could not answer me!

Suddenly, the demon spirit shouted the girl's name and said, "She is dead, she is dead." Also, the spirit told me that the girl would die within one year. That spirit was an absolute liar though because that girl is still alive today!

Because I was so afraid that day, I assumed that no one in the conference would be touched by the power of God. However, God's power in that conference was so strong that even the ushers who were standing outside the building fell down by the power of God. Since then, I have seen the Holy Spirit moving tremendously in healing people.

JOY AND PEACE

The Holy Spirit brings joy and peace in our lives. Even His rebuke will bring peace and joy. When the Holy Spirit sets us free from darkness, this brings us joy, and not fear. If you have an experience that confuses you and makes you more and more fearful, then it is best to consider praying again to the Holy Spirit. Ask Him to help you. Remember, the Bible says, "But the fruit of the Spirit is love, joy, peace, patience, kindness, goodness, faithfulness, gentleness and self-control" (Gal. 5:22).

If the fruit of the Holy Spirit are these things, it means He also has these qualities. It would be impossible for Him to give us patience if He Himself is not patient, or for Him to give us peace if He Himself has no peace in Him. When He is in a situation, then the fruit will be His own character.

THE BIBLE STUDIES GREW

In the days when I was having Bible studies with Joseph, I never intended to be a full-time preacher of the gospel. I did it because I wanted to help Joseph. Many times I heard that I must work for the Lord, but back then I was a businessman and at the same time working toward my doctorate at the university. My plan was to make money and support the body of Christ through financial means. Joseph was the only person I was teaching.

I had a business partner named John. We worked together almost every day. I used to talk to him about God. Many times we had discussions and arguments. He was stubborn just like I had been before I was born again. He used to argue that there is no God and that we came into existence through evolution. He knew a lot about science and he did not want to know anything other than that. He did not want religion, but he had forgotten that even science is a type of modern religion. He always told me that in religion, you believe things without seeing, and in science you see it first. But this statement was not true because there are also many things in the sciences that are just accepted and assumed, such as the theory of evolution.

Because no one could have possibly been there in the beginning, even the evolution theory requires faith in something that no one saw or experienced. John's assumption was obviously untrue because the theory requires having faith in something he did not see or experience. As for me, I made it clear to him that if I have to choose which one I want to believe, I will certainly choose that I am from God and not from a type of monkey. John and I would always argue about these scientific issues.

What about you? Where did you begin? Where did you come from?

IN THE BEGINNING

Genesis is the first book of the Holy Bible. "Genesis" is a Greek word that means "origin or source." In the original Hebrew, this book is titled as Bereshith, *which means "in the beginning." God is our beginning. It is God who created this world. The Book of Genesis, chapter one, teaches us that the beginning of everything starts with God.*

Let me give you an example: In our world today, there are many children who have identity problems. They do not know who their fathers or mothers are. When they grow up, they have psychological problems because they do not know who their biological parents are. They end up having serious problems or even committing suicide. The same is true about our society today—it has forgotten Who its real Father is, and Who is its beginning. *This is why our cities are sick—struggling with hatred, adultery, anger, wars, poverty, criminality and the like.*

When people start to ignore God as the beginning of everything, they will then start to also ignore the commandments of God, the Beginner. They will ignore the teachings of God's prophets, His Word and His Son, Jesus Christ. When they choose to ignore God, then their children will not be raised according to His plan, thus, resulting in a chaotic family, chaotic society and a chaotic world.

This is the reason why children turn to drugs and families break up. Men have ignored the beginning: God as the Creator. When a person knows his beginning, no one can deceive him. When you know your beginning, you also know your present and your end. You know where you are going. The Bible teaches us that in the beginning there was already the triune God. Jesus Christ already existed when God was creating our world:

> In the beginning was the Word, and the Word was with God and the Word was God. He [Jesus] was with God in the beginning. Through him all things were made; without him [Jesus] nothing was made that has been made.
> —John 1:1–3

Jesus also said, "I tell you the truth, before Abraham was born, I am!" (John 8:58). This means we cannot know our God, our beginning, unless we know Jesus. The difference between Jews and Christians is that Jews do not believe that Jesus Christ is God. You cannot know your beginning without believing, knowing and obeying the teachings of Jesus.

Further, in the beginning was (is) the Holy Spirit. Genesis 1:2 says that the Spirit of God was hovering over the waters. We cannot know our Father without knowing His Spirit. We must acknowledge the existence of the Holy Spirit and obey His voice, because He is our Counselor and Teacher at this moment.

CREATION OF MEN

In Genesis 1 we read that God first created the heavens and the earth. Then He created the light and the separation of waters, and He created the plants and animals, from the smallest to the biggest. After the earth was ready, God made man. God gave all these things to man and told him to rule over them. Like parents who are expecting the birth of their child, they make ready the child's room, the child's dress and the child's bed during this nine-month period. Then when the child is born, everything is ready and his room has been prepared. Everything was ready for man when God created him. Genesis 2 describes the creation of man. "The Lord God formed the man from the dust of the ground and breathed into his nostrils the breath of life, and the man became a living being" (Gen. 2:7). Despite this, mankind continues his quest in looking for his origin, how he came into the world as a human being. So, who is a human being actually?

First, a human being is created in the image of God. God created man in His own image. Evolutionists tell us that we are an advanced form of the intelligent kind of monkey. They tell us that we came from monkeys, that our forefathers are monkeys. This is wrong because God made us in His own image. Contrary to this, we just learned that God breathed His breath into man. Breath in Hebrew is neshamah, *which means "energy, wind or spirit." God made us in a special way.*

God is the greatest Artist. Think of this: You are very beautiful artwork made by God. God enjoys His artwork when He sees you because He loves you the way He made you. You are a unique person with a unique body and characteristics. You are God's special handiwork. In all the world there is no one quite like you. This is very pleasant in God's eyes.

Secondly, because of man's likeness to God, he or she is a moral being. Every man and woman knows what is good and what is bad. Even nonbelievers know these things because man was made in the image of God. I believe that there is something good even in the heart of a criminal.

Thirdly, a man is a rational being because God is also rational. Our God is the Creator, and in the same way, we are creative beings. Look at our world now; human beings have achieved tremendous technological, scientific and artistic goals. Man flies. Man discovers. Man makes. All these are possible because man is made in the image of God.

Fourthly, a human being is an eternal being because God is eternal. But after the fall of man, sin came to this world and man became mortal in his flesh. However, man is still an eternal spiritual being. The Bible says that after death there are two kinds of life: The eternal peaceful life in heaven, and the eternal life that is filled with gnashing of teeth, condemnation and punishment. Those who believe and obey God the Father, Jesus Christ and the Holy Spirit will live forever in eternal peace and joy.

> *Jesus said, "I am the resurrection and the life. He who believes in me will live, even though he dies; and whoever lives and believes in me will never die" (John 11:25–26).*
>
> *Lastly, a human being is an authority being with free will. God created this world, and He appointed Adam to rule over it. He also gave Adam free will. If God did not give us free will, we would be like robots. He gave us free will so that we can choose Him or not. He even gave us the free will to reject and ignore Him. We, as human beings, have ignored God, His teachings and His commandments by rejecting Jesus Christ as our Savior. We have abused our God-given authority and our free will, and we have messed up our world. That is why we have wars and the destruction of the environment.*

The Street Lamp

I remember how my business partner, John, came to Christ. I had always prayed for him, never giving up on him. John was not only my partner, he was also my neighbor. We used to walk together every night to talk business and get some fresh air. But one night I was so filled with the Holy Spirit that I could not stop talking about God. I told him that when God is with us, nothing can be against us.

Believe it or not, just as I was telling him that God will protect us, at that very moment someone threw down huge amounts of water from an apartment to try to hit us. It was already midnight, and the water only missed hitting us by only two centimeters.

The experience shocked John. As we walked down further, a lady opened the window, cursed and spit on us. But the spit also did not touch us. We came back to the main street where there was a damaged street lamp. The lamp was 100 percent out. At that moment I could hear what John was saying in his heart. He said, "If Sam's God is a real God, if Jesus is real, let Sam command the lamp to shine." I looked at John, and I asked him why he doubted. I also told him that if he wanted me to do it, he must ask me. He was surprised at how I could "hear" the things in his heart. Then I looked at the lamp and said, "In the name of Jesus Christ, the Son of God, shine." Suddenly, the lamp shone in the darkness.

John jumped. "How did you do that?" he asked. But then he said, "Tell the lamp to go off again." Then I looked at the lamp and commanded it go out. Immediately, the lamp went out. John asked me to do it again, and I did that. That night John gave his life to Christ. Shortly after, his wife gave her life to Christ. Today they are members of the executive board of Jesus Christ Foundation World Evangelism. John is also the leader of the music ministry.

John, Joseph and I now travel together all over the world, glorifying Jesus Christ as Lord and Savior.

> *Yes, just like that lamp, God can turn every darkness to light. God is light. If your life is in darkness, do not worry! Darkness never wins over light. Goodness never loses to evil. Sickness never wins over the healing which is in Jesus Christ. If your life is hopeless, if it seems headed in the wrong way or if you are praying for someone you love to come back to the Lord, do not lose heart: Light always triumphs over darkness. Truth always wins over lies; goodness always wins over wrong. There is nothing impossible with God. You and I do not need to live under the curse. We are somebody—sons and daughters of God.*

MY MINISTRY STARTED

After John and his wife were converted, I now had three people in my Bible studies. Every Tuesday we tried to learn, and I started to become a little experienced at it.

One day I had this strange experience. My mother-in-law phoned to tell me about a woman who wanted to be prayed for. She asked me to come to her house to pray for the woman. I was so tired that day that I almost said no to her. But once again a voice in me told me to go. It was the voice of my Teacher, the Holy Spirit. He said, "Go and I will be with you." I took my bike and went to my in-law's house.

As the lady sat there, she would not look at my face. She somehow opposed everything I told her. I was not comfortable with her. I told her, "Let me pray for you." I laid my hand on her shoulders and started to pray. The minute I mentioned the name of Lord Jesus, she jumped up, her face changed and her voice changed into a man's voice. The voice said, "What do you want from me?" The voice was a demon inside the woman. The demon said, "I know you, you are from Jesus. He was with the Father from the beginning. Don't cast me out please. I want to kill this woman."

It took me more than five hours to cast out the demon. Then the lady began to pray in tongues and started to bow down before me! I thought, *Why is she bowing before me?* Later she told me that she saw Jesus in me. The woman's sickness was also healed. After that, people started to ask me to pray for them. Many came to Christ and were healed. Some traveled 500 kilometers to receive their healing in Jesus' name. Many were saved and brought into the kingdom. We had revival meetings right in my house and we experienced wonderful things. Signs and wonders followed my ministry. In the beginning, it was easy to evangelize people. Every time I spoke to people, they easily gave their lives to Christ. I wondered how this was possible. I did not know that those I brought into the kingdom at that time would one day form a powerful team that would reach the world with the gospel of Jesus Christ.

I REJECTED GOD'S VOICE

Human beings are some of the most stubborn and disobedient creatures in the world; and I am one of them. I could see God's power in my life. I could see His might and blessings, but I still did not want to be a full-time minister of the gospel. I had known my calling in my heart from the time the Lord had called me into His kingdom, but I was still hearing other words. I was still holding on to many things in life.

Just imagine, I planned to be a Third-World expert by studying in a university, and I had high-level business opportunities; and then suddenly, God came into my life and changed the direction of my life 180 degrees. And so there I was, rejecting His plan and still wanting to go my own way.

However, God knows how to handle us. He lets us go our own way, but without His blessing. And so I did the things I wanted to do, especially the business. But I did them without His blessings! I tried to escape from His plan. He let me go, but He knew that this particular son of His would come back to Him.

My business started going wrong. I had powerful plans and wonderful orders. I remember John and I were to have a business meeting with one of the biggest telecommunication companies. Their business could have brought us huge amounts of monthly income. We were supposed to meet with their president, a very busy woman who had sacrificed her time to meet with us personally. However, something unexpected happened. As John and I were driving a car to our appointment with the president, the car broke down. Because of this mishap, we were late for this very important appointment, and when we finally arrived, the secretary told us that the president no longer wanted to see us because we were late. She also told us to forget the business we had with that company.

We were very disappointed! We went to a coffee shop, and I said to John, "Look, I do not want to go into business again. I want to continue with my studies, finish it and do a little work for God." John was disappointed, but he agreed. So I gave up my business plans and my so-called bright, rich future.

There was a second thing in my life with which God wanted to deal: my studies. I was an average student at the university. I was not that excellent, but not that bad either. But since I did not obey God's voice, things also went wrong in my studies—my grades dropped. Even though I was studying hard, my grades were not even good enough to pass. Something was wrong, but I did not know what it was. I did not realize it was because I was disobeying God.

> *Disobeying God never blesses us; it only brings confusion and disappointment. Are you obeying God? Did God ask you to do something but you didn't do it? Is what you are doing now from God, or from your own fleshly motives? If God has blessed you in doing what you are doing, you will be successful and achieve many things in spite of difficulties and challenges. We can know that God is behind what we are doing if He helps us during times of difficulties and challenges. Difficulties and challenges will still come to pass, but God will help us and use them to make us into better people. Never try to run away from challenges and troubles, but face them. When God's blessing is upon what you are doing, He will use the challenges to build you up.*
>
> *However, when God is not behind what you are doing, sooner or later the challenges and difficulties will burn you out! Obeying God is crucial.*

OBEYING OR DISOBEYING

These days, everyone is after the blessings. Everyone wants happiness and security. Some people try to secure their lives with insurance, but still they don't feel secure. When natural disasters come and kill thousands of lives, insurance does not guarantee safety or security.

Some people put their trust in having a lot of money and possessions, yet deep in their hearts, they are neither happy nor contented. They may spend their time in expensive restaurants or gambling in casinos, thinking perhaps that they could find security and blessings there, but deep down they are still insecure and living in fear of losing what they have. They have no peace because they are constantly wracking their brains trying to think of ways to make more money and get more possessions.

TRUE BLESSINGS

What then, is the answer to this lack of security and blessings? Let me ask you these simple questions: Are you blessed in your life? If yes, in what way? How do you measure your blessings? How did you gain them?

Before starting on this fantastic spiritual journey with you, let us agree that the source of blessing is not money, material things or possessions. The only source of blessings is a divine power. This is not the power of black magic, the power of some voodoo man, of Chukka, Pokka or Abracadabra. The only way to receive blessing is through the divine power of God.

Many people ask very familiar questions such as: If God exists, why then do we face so many problems in our homes? Why do we have conflicts among people? Why do we have chaos in our cities and in our countries? Why do we have so many natural disasters today?

God is good and never intended to bring disaster or calamity in your life, or in any person's life. God does not want us to live a life of condemnations and sufferings. Please, never say that God is not good. Maybe the system is not good, maybe we human beings are not good, but God is good!

Look at the world. Shall we blame God for what is happening in our world today? Will you blame Him because people kill and destroy one another?

If you read and look back at the history of human beings, you will see that it was human beings who made guns and gunpowder and used them for killing one another. Human beings abused innocent children, raped them and used them for child pornography. Please don't tell me that all these things happen because of God! No! These results were from disobedient men and their choices to be out of God's plan and purpose! God did not choose to kill; man chose to kill! God gave us love, but we chose hate. God gave us blessings, but the world chose cursing instead.

"Now it shall come to pass, if you diligently obey the voice of the LORD your God, to observe carefully all His commandments which I command you today, the LORD your God will set you high above all nations on earth" (Deut. 28:1, NKJV).

This scripture reveals what God promised to the Jews when they were delivered from Egypt and on their way to the Promised Land.

This same passage speaks to us today. It asks us to obey the voice of God and observe His commandments. Since we are now in the New Covenant time, the voice of God is Jesus Christ Himself and His Holy Spirit. There is no other voice of God except the voice of Jesus. Never believe those people who ask you for money to bring you in contact with other powers. Although the powers may be supernatural, they are the dark powers. They will do what you ask them to do but will later bring you under a curse.

But believing in Jesus Christ is not enough. You

must live as Christ lived. God confirmed His contract of blessings to us through a promise in Deuteronomy 28:2. "All these blessings will come and overtake you, because you obey the voice of the Lord your God." What are these blessings that God promised us if we obey Him? Allow me to explain. God always makes Himself clear and His words are faultless. He has no secret codes or secret language, but is upright and clear.

Deuteronomy 28 is the chapter on blessings that God promised to those who will obey His voice, Jesus Christ, and observe His commandments. The following will happen if you obey Him:

1. YOU WILL BE BLESSED IN THE CITY AND COUNTRY

"Blessed shall you be in the city, and blessed shall you be in the country" (Deut. 28:3, NKJV).

In these days, our cities are under a great curse! Crime is on the rise. In addition, thefts, robberies, accidents, drug addiction and other crimes mark our cities. But we cannot blame God for this state of affairs. For example, in many countries, carnivals are associated with sexual immoralities, alcohol and drug use.

Some people try to escape from one city to another or go from one country to another. Some come to Europe in hopes of a better life, but sometimes their lives become even worse than before. However, do not worry, because the Bible says that you will be blessed in the city and in the country where you go. Whether you are in Amsterdam, Cape Town, New York or wherever, God's blessings will be upon you if you hear and obey His voice. Maybe you need blessings in the city where you live right now, or maybe you just came to this country. God is calling you through His Son, Jesus. Do not miss the chance to be blessed.

2. YOU WILL BE BLESSED IN YOUR FAMILY LIFE

"Blessed shall be the fruit of your body (womb) . . ." (Deut. 28:4, NKJV).

In this day and age, fathers and mothers are filled with sorrow because of their children's disobedience. Some of their children are on alcohol and drugs, and many of them have gone astray and are confused. However, the youth are disobedient because the majority of their parents disobey God. The Bible has given us a promise concerning our family, and He is faithful to His promises. But, if fathers and mothers cannot obey God, how can they expect their children to obey them?

While married couples suffer as a result of their children, others are in distress because they cannot bear children. They have tried many doctors and have spent thousands and thousands of dollars to have a child, but to no avail. The Bible says clearly that the fruit of your womb will be blessed. Jesus Christ healed the sick and made the dead rise from grave. The Bible mentions the barren woman whose womb was miraculously touched by God, and she gave birth. If you are barren, do not give up hope. Continue to obey God's commands. Everything is possible for those who believe and obey the commands of our living Lord Jesus Christ.

3. HE WILL GRANT YOU ABUNDANT PROSPERITY

"Blessed shall be your basket and your kneading bowl" (Deut. 28:5, NKJV).

Many people do not know where their money goes when they receive their income. Some must pay so many bills that they never have enough money. Others live under crushing poverty. In fact, in some countries 8 out of 10 people live below the poverty line.

But, our Father promised us that if we would only obey His commands then our baskets will be filled. God never wanted us to suffer poverty. He made this world and gave everything to us. He is a good God. The only thing He wants from us is our obedience.

I have known people who began to experience abundant blessings from the moment they began to obey and worship God and His Son, Jesus Christ. I met a person who had many problems in his life. His father and mother were divorced. He could not study well and was expelled from school. He thought of running away from home, as he was also an illegal person in Europe. His friends brought him to me, and I started to preach the gospel to him and the beauty of God's love for us. He gave his life to Jesus Christ and was touched by the power of the Holy Spirit. He felt like a new person. The only talent he had was playing football.

One week later, he came to the church to bid us goodbye because one of the most famous football teams in Germany offered him a great contract. God has blessed him enormously.

4. THE LORD WILL BLESS YOU WHEN YOU COME IN AND WHEN YOU GO OUT (DEUT. 28:6)

Many people enjoy their lives outside their homes. They enjoy their wonderful jobs and the company of their colleagues, but their homes are like hell. They have problems with either their spouse or their children. Other people are the opposite and are very blessed at home but quite tragic at their place of work. These individuals may have problems either with their colleagues or boss, and work seems like hell.

The Bible clearly states that God promises to bless you no matter where you are or whatever you are doing, but you must obey Him.

5. YOUR ENEMIES WILL BE DEFEATED (DEUT. 28:7)

The Bible promised us that if we obey Him then our enemies will be defeated. We live in a world filled with enemies and think that our enemies are those we come in contact with every day in our lives. But, that concept is a big mistake, because the Bible says that we must love our enemies and bless them. Jesus Christ loved the sinners but hated the sin; He loved the sick but hated the sickness. The enemies I am referring to are the dark powers and the unseen forces that keep you away from your blessings. There are powers that bring curses into your lives, and this is bad news for all of us. However, the good news of the gospel of Christ declares that every curse will be broken if a person comes to Jesus Christ and obeys Him. By the death and the Resurrection of Jesus Christ, the spiritual enemy has been defeated. Christ has dominion over the devil, and because Jesus is in you, you have the same power as He has. Is cancer your enemy? Then worry not, because it can be healed. Is tuberculosis your enemy? It can also be healed. Are there problems in your family? They can be solved!

6. EVERYTHING YOU PUT YOUR HAND TO WILL BE BLESSED

"The Lord will command the blessing on you in your storehouses and in all to which you set your hand . . ." (Deut. 28:8, NKJV).

The Bible grants us the power that everything on which we put our hands will be blessed. Please focus on the word everything (all). 'Everything' means every project, every plan or every decision you might make will be fulfilled and will be blessed if they are in the Lord's will.

When I was a little boy, I desired to have a magic stick so that whatever I would touch would turn into gold. Unfortunately, that was not possible. However, I have found a much greater and much better power than the magic stick that I desired as a child. That is the power of Christ. You may be starting a business, looking for a job or planning a marriage. One way to be successful in these endeavors is to obey the voice of God through His Holy Spirit.

7. THE LORD WILL MAKE YOU THE HEAD AND NOT THE TAIL (DEUT. 28:13)

God made us and has intended for us to live a life

like kings. He never created us to live under the pressure and dominion of darkness, but many people still live under the shadow of an inferiority complex. They think that they are inferior because of their shape, color, language or status in life.

But, the good news of the gospel is that you are unique and special. Jesus Christ believes in your abilities. He knows you are the most worthy person for Him. You do not need to end up in a psychiatric institution or hospital. You are special and beautiful. You are able and worthy. You are the head and not the tail. Trust in God and trust in yourself. God gave you two ways to choose, the way to blessing or the way to curse. Which one will you choose? There are two groups of people in the world, those who are blessed and those who are cursed. To which group do you want to belong?

THE SINFUL CHOICE

When God created Adam and Eve, He gave them the right to eat from the fruit of any tree, except from the tree that was in the middle of the garden. God provided the chance to choose whether to obey Him and not eat from the fruit or to disobey Him and eat the forbidden fruit. God gave men free will to choose between obeying or disobeying Him. By giving them the rule to not eat the fruit of the tree in the middle of the garden, God gave man a choice.

God also told Adam what the result would be if he ate from the tree.

> *And the woman said to the serpent,*
> *"We may eat fruit from the trees in the*
> *garden, but God did say, 'You must not*
> *eat from the tree that is in the middle of*
> *the garden, and you must not touch it, or*
> *you will die.'"*
>
> —GENESIS 3:2–3

The same situation happens in our world today because God gives us a chance to choose. Shall we choose to love or to hate? Shall we choose war or peace? Most of the time horrible things happen in the world because people make wrong choices.

For example, God did not create people to hate each other, but on contrary, He created them for love. God never created this world to give us a miserable life. The source of misery is when we make the wrong choices. God is again putting us in situations where we can choose to obey Him and believe in His Son Jesus Christ or to reject Him and live according to our own rules and regulations. Jesus said in John 6:45–47,

> *Everyone who listens to the Father and learns from him comes to me. No one has seen the Father except the one who is from God; only he has seen the Father. I tell you the truth he who believes has everlasting life.*

The will of God for us is to have eternal life, which only comes through His Son Jesus Christ. In addition,

the will of God is that we live a holy life according to His will and to the teachings of Jesus Christ.
Romans 12:1–2 says:

> *Therefore, I urge you, brothers, in view of God's mercy, to offer your bodies as living sacrifice, holy and pleasing to God—this is your spiritual act of worship. Do not conform any longer to the patterns of this world, but be transformed by the renewing of your mind. Then you will be able to test and approve what God's will is—his good, pleasing and perfect will.*

Now look at the contrast. In Genesis 3:3 God told Adam to not eat from the fruits of that specific tree, and in Romans 12:1–3 God said to us today, "do not be conformed to the patterns of this world." These two instructions are the same.

The patterns of this world are: dishonesty, hate, lies, orgies, drunkenness, drugs, gossip, fighting, sexual immorality. Do not have anything to do with them and do not even touch them, for in Genesis 3:3 God said to not touch the tree.

DO NOT TOUCH

God does not want us to touch or to come near the patterns of the world. Never forget that touch *is the beginning of* temptation, *and temptation is the beginning of sin. Sin is the start of* fall *and* death. *If you do not want to fall like Adam and Eve and do not want sin in your life, then stop touching, meeting, or having things in your life that cause you to sin and to fall. Let me give you an example:*

God said that we should avoid getting drunk. God hates it. If you are around friends who drink too much alcohol, then you are actually in touch with them. Sooner or later they will most likely cause you to sin and get drunk. God said avoid sexual immoralities among you. Nowadays many things happen that are not according the will of God: a man sleeps with man, a woman lays with a woman, a man abuses children, and a mother abuses daughters sexually. Do you know why? One of the reasons is the television. It is filled with junk and dirty things. As people look at these things, they become more crazy and pass it along to their children. As a Christian, if you watch TV channels in your house that display too much sex or violence, then you are in touch with these things. Before things of this nature tempt you, block the channels from your television in order to avoid anything that brings temptation. Do not even go near it.

THE TEMPTATION

Touch is the start of temptation. *In Genesis 3:4–5, we read that the woman saw that the fruit of the tree was good for food, pleasing to the eye, and also desirable for gaining wisdom. The woman saw first, which means that she was near the tree. Symbolically, this can be 'the touch.'*

After the "touch" she saw that tree was good for many things, which is the temptation. As with Eve, the devil tempts us in three ways:

1. Good for food
2. Pleasing to the eyes
3. Desirable for gaining wisdom

Good for food *is one of the biggest temptations of human beings. Because of food, people kill and destroy each other. Because of food, they sin and hate. In our life we can apply "food" not only to food itself but also to money, possessions and wealth. Do not let these things tempt you so that you become blind and cannot see the will of God.*

In Matthew 4:1–11, the devil tempted Jesus with food. He came to Jesus and told Him to command the stones to become bread so that He could eat and fall. But, Jesus rejected the tempter and said, "It is written, 'Man shall not live by bread alone, but by every word that comes from the mouth of God.'"

Pleasing to the eyes *is the second temptation that Eve received. She saw that the fruits are very pleasing to the eyes. There are things in our daily lives that please the eyes, but they are dangerous and can make us fall. Drugs seem pleasing to your eyes but are dangerous. Illicit sex seem pleasing to the eyes but is dangerous. Money seems pleasing to the eyes but is dangerous.*

Pleasure seems good for the eyes but can destroy your life. The beautiful cigarette advertisements with their big posters and beautiful box in eye-catching colors are pleasing to the eye. Even if you are not a smoker, you can be tempted to buy and try. And once you start smoking, it is difficult to stop.

Yes, the devil knows that one of the weaknesses of human beings is the "pleased eyes." That is why there are so many TV advertisements for the products, which seem very pleasing but are actually dangerous for us.

> The lips of an adulteress drip honey, and her speech is smoother that oil, but in the end she is bitter as gall, sharp as a double-edged sword. Her feet go down to death; her steps lead straight to grave.
> —Proverbs 5:2–5

Desire for wisdom *is another big temptation that man can face. Human beings have always desired to know more. Nothing is wrong with this, but if we try to put our knowledge above God's wisdom, then we are going toward destruction. God has given us knowledge to glorify Him, not to deny Him. Because of so much technology, science, and human wisdom, we even deny the existence of God. Because of so much technology and science, we say there is no God and that the human being is God. For this reason, God will destroy the wisdom of the wise and confuse the philosophers of the world who claim that there is no God. (Read 1 Corinthians 1:1–26.)*

THE SIN AND THE FALL

After the temptation, we read in Genesis 3:3 that the woman took the fruit and ate it. She sinned, tempted Adam, and allowed him to eat the fruit also. Yes, Eve could have avoided sinning from the beginning if she stopped coming near the tree (the touch). She could have also stopped during the temptation. But no, she became blind because of the three temptations, and she sinned. Let us live a holy life and avoid any unholy touch and temptation by our own strong will and by the help of the Holy Spirit. If there is something around you that causes you to be tempted, throw it away before you fall.

We read in Genesis 3 that God became angry with Adam and Eve and judged them. In verses 3:8–12, we see that God asked Adam three major questions:

1. *Where are you? (v. 9)*
2. *Who told you that you are naked? (v. 11)*
3. *Have you eaten? What have you done? (v. 11)*

God is going to ask these three questions of every sinner who does not believe in Jesus Christ. Believers are forgiven, but for unbelievers, God is going to ask them these questions and hear their answers.

God is asking, "Where are you?" to every human being. Yes, we are in the middle of a miserable world filled with hatred and war. Human beings have messed up this world because of their sinful activities.

God is asking us, "Where are you?" Are we in Jesus Christ or are we in the world? Have you asked this question of yourself?

Furthermore, God will ask them, "Who told you to sin?" or "Why did you listen to others?" Temptation comes always from someone or from something else. For Eve, it came from the serpent. For Adam, it came from Eve. Maybe for you it can enter through your friends or the television or any other things. Avoid them.

Lastly, God will ask the sinners, "Did you sin?" or, "What have you done?" This means that we are responsible for our actions, for one day everyone in the world must give an account to the one who created them, the Lord.

I MADE UP MY MIND

Everything in my life went wrong at once. I lost my business, and my declining grades brought stress and sadness. The following question came to my mind: *Why me, Lord? There are millions of people, why did you choose me, Lord?* One day in April 1995, I was alone at home watching CNN. They were showing some disaster scenes.

The Lord spoke in my heart, not in an audible voice but a whisper. He asked me, "If you had all the certificates and all the titles in the world, will they bring you salvation and everlasting life?"

I answered, "No!"

Then He asked me, "If you had all the money in the world, will you enter heaven with them?"

Again, I answered, "No!"

He told me that it is better to obey Him because there are hundreds of people who need me in order to be saved!

I fell on my knees and said, "Lord, I am so sorry. I give up fighting with You. Beginning today, I will choose Your plan. I will obey You and be a full-time minister!"

Chapter 5

The Adventures Began

O N THAT APRIL DAY WHEN I GOT ON MY KNEES AND repented of my disobedience, the Spirit of God immediately came upon me and told me, "Stand up; go to this certain place in the city. There is a building. You will take it, and next Sunday you will have your first official service." I knew back then that it was difficult to find even a small place to worship in the town where I lived, so I answered, "But Lord, it is difficult to find a building here!" The Lord said to me, "That is My problem and not yours. The only thing you need to do is to obey what I told you." I agreed and left home and went to the street where God told me to go. He told me that when I arrived there He would let me know which building it was. But honestly, I could not find anything; there were many buildings there.

I went in one of the buildings and asked the man in

charge if we could rent their place. The man told me that they prefer to rent out the place for dancing and other parties but not to Christian groups.

Next, I went to a reformed church and asked them if they wanted to rent out the place to me. They asked, "What kind of church are you?" I told them by saying, "We are a born-again church." The man did not understand what I meant and rejected me. Disappointed, I decided to return home. I thought I was fooling myself. Why did I go out of the house? Maybe it was not God who told me to go and look for a building. But while walking, I passed by this building that was closed and dark inside. The voice of the Lord said, "This is the building." I replied, "But Lord, this building is old and closed." The Lord said, "Go in, and there is a man inside." I went in and indeed there was this old man there. I said to the man, "I am from church. Can I rent this building from you?" He said, "Yes, I have two classrooms upstairs. On Sunday we are closed, so you can use the rooms." I asked him when I could begin using them, and he told me this Sunday.

The following day was Friday so I went back to the man and signed the contract. We had our first service that Sunday with five people.

I preached in English because God told me to do so. He said that He wanted to use me internationally so I must preach in English, and my church must be an international church. We only had eight members, my wife and I, my mother-in-law, John, his wife, Joseph, a Korean brother and his wife.

My friends said, "We are only eight people here, but you sound as if you are preaching to five thousand! Cool down, please!" Our first service was fun.

PERSECUTIONS

When my mother and father heard that I had become a preacher, they were shocked. They started to persecute me. My father threatened to take away my inheritance. My mother did not talk to me for awhile. Every time I visited them, my mother would pick a fight with me. I went through terrible times and nightmares. But, I had made up my mind, and nobody could stop me. One of my friends came to my house and told me, "Look at you! A so-called man of God, but you do not have even enough money to buy a good TV set." He was so filled with pride.

The Bible says that pride always comes before a fall. Two weeks later, the same man who mocked me went bankrupt.

We may have all the money in the world and yet live a life of misery. We can be proud of what we are in the eyes of the world, but still suffer deep inside. It is not the world's wealth that makes us happy and successful.

No, only Jesus can give us peace, joy and security in life. The things of the world belong to the world. None of them will be able to save us. Of course, I do not mean that we must reject blessing and wealth. No! Not at all, but we must choose for Jesus Christ in all circumstances.

Whether we are poor, sick, rich, healthy, powerless or powerful, in all situations let us depend on Christ our Lord. *Persecutions will always follow us once we choose to follow God's plan in our life.* People mocked me and made jokes behind my back. I lost some friends simply because I chose Jesus and His work. Once I heard people gossiping behind me saying things like, "Sam has become crazy. He says that he is a prophet and is Jesus." People talked behind my back, but I did not care, because I had a purpose in life—*to preach the gospel.*

CHRISTIAN PERSECUTIONS

As the news spread that I had become a preacher, not only did my countrymen and family members persecute me, but my fellow Christian brothers and sisters also persecuted me. One time I was invited to visit a group of Asian pastors and evangelists from Los Angeles. As we were eating, they asked me by whose authority did I do these things. They asked me where were my theological diplomas. They told me that I needed to get a Ph.D. degree to heal people. I was hurt.

When I came home, I was so upset that I told God I was going to quit because these men were right. That night I slept alone on the living room couch. It was four in the morning when I began to hear the sounds of birds outside. I asked myself who would wake these little birds in the middle of the night? Suddenly, there was a great and mighty wind in my room. I could sense the presence of three people in the room, but I could not see them. One of the men called me by name and said, "Jesus has sent us to tell you that you must go on with your work, for God is behind you. Jesus is standing behind you." I grew afraid at that moment. I asked for the man's name. He said he was Elijah and the other one was Moses. It wasn't clear to me whether or not the third person was Elisha. I woke up that day and made up my mind that I was in a battle and must stand firm. I decided to be stronger through all these persecutions. God is looking for people who hear His voice and obey.

WHOSE VOICE DO YOU HEAR?

Today we hear so many voices that we are confused about whom to believe and whom not to believe, whom to

84

follow and not to follow. Most of the time our personalities are dependent on what we hear and who we hear or follow in life. We are mostly influenced by culture, society and what people around us think or say about us.

Culture, society and environment have many voices. For example, I know many frustrated young people who were forced by their parents to study something that they did not want to or to become something that they did not like. Their parents believed that if their children studied law or medicine then they would be able to earn more money. They believed that having more money would lead them to having more things and living a more luxurious life. However, those parents forgot that education is not about achieving a higher social status or earning more money to have more things. Instead, the purpose of education is to train and encourage young people to reach their potential so that they can serve the Lord through their talents and abilities.

I experienced this problem myself. My family wanted me to be someone that God did not call me to be. Because of this, I had to make a choice between the two. I am neither a medical doctor nor a professor in the secular college, because that is not my nature. I am a preacher of the simple gospel message, and in that I am successful and blessed. Please do not misunderstand me. Of course, we must direct our children and guide them toward a better future, but we must also give room for the Lord to do what He wants to do with our children for His perfect purpose and plan.

Now, I am not saying that everybody should be a preacher. Maybe someone is called to be a doctor, a car engineer or a pilot, because that is what God desires of that person.

> *Whose voice do you hear today? Do you hear the voice of your culture and tradition? Do you hear the voice of the people around you? Jesus said, "My sheep know my voice." Hear His voice because that is the safest way. He will be with you whenever you cross the sea of difficulties.*

DIFFICULT TIMES

The early period of my ministry was not an easy time. Not only was I persecuted by other Christians and by family members, but I was also forced to prove myself to my own church members. After studying hard and writing a sermon in English that I later preached, I used to hear comments like, "Your English has improved," or "This week your English was not so good." I used to get hurt and would argue with them. I would say to them that God does not look at how professionally you speak, but rather on how you obey Him. Sometimes when we had Bible studies, no one would come except my wife. I would go after the church members and beg them to come and follow Christ. Sometimes I would even argue with them, but God gave me a patient heart to deal with them and pray for them. Thanks to God, today all of them are part of my team.

They are now mature Christians and are standing behind me in the work of the Lord. In all these difficult times, I had only one closest friend, the Holy Spirit, Whom I love and respect deeply and after Him, my lovely wife, Sarah.

GROWTH AND DECLINE

The way I organized the church was quite conservative. I did not practice any healing during the service or laying hands on people because I was afraid of offending people or being misunderstood by them. My church grew to fifteen members back then. One day, the Spirit of God came on me and said, "Lay your hands on people and pray for them and heal them. Do not listen to people." The next morning it was Sunday, and I laid my hands on people. Signs and wonders followed, but that day we lost almost all the members except for the team, all of which were refreshed and revived. We were again down to eight people. Then the Lord said to me, "Now I, the Lord, will use you." Go out from this church building, and I will give you a new one.

Do you recall the Korean church where my wife had worshiped and the place I had planned to set on fire when I was not yet in the Lord? Well, that church had moved to the USA.

The owner of the building dreamed that Jesus visited him and said, "Rent the church to my son, Samuel Lee." There were many interested tenants, and there I was with fifty dollars in the church account proposing to rent the place for eight hundred dollars. I was doubting, but in the Lord I took the bold step and rented the building. People asked me how we could do this without any money, and yet we rented this building that required both money and repairs. Believe it or not, with that fifty dollars we painted and repaired the whole place. Slowly the church grew; many Africans, Filipinos and Asians joined the church. My audience changed the way I preached; I nearly became a black preacher. Upon seeing me, many people cannot believe that I came from the Middle East.

However, people who heard me on radio thought I was an African. I thank God for the congregation that He gave me.

The church grew. We needed chairs so I prayed to God for a hundred more. Within two days, in a mysterious way, we had 110 chairs placed free of charge outside the church door. A brother helped get those chairs. The church started to grow, but the Lord had a different plan for me and for the church.

SOMEONE GOT SAVED

In the church we had a Filipino sister, Myrna, who joined our ministry team. Myrna had a Catholic sister who worked as a domestic helper in Cyprus. The sister in Cyprus was suffering because of work pressure and family problems. She was losing hope. When Myrna told me about her sister, God spoke to my heart saying, "My son, take the audio cassette recorder and evangelize her. Address the cassette to her personally." I took the audio recorder and taped a personal message for her. Together with my testimony, I explained to her how I received Christ. I also prayed for her in that tape.

We mailed the cassette and a few weeks later she received it. When she heard the cassette, she started crying and at the same time was filled with the Holy Spirit and gave her life to Christ. When she gave the cassette to another sister, the same thing happened to her. She got saved, and within a month, a group of new converts who received Christ through the cassette was formed. I then visited Cyprus and blessed them. They became the second church that was formed under my ministry. Today, this same church in Cyprus is reaching many people around the world, sharing the gospel and bringing fruit to God's kingdom.

I am always amazed at how God moves in ways we could never imagine. A cassette valued at two dollars brought forth a new church and a mission center in another country. I just shared my testimony, and these sisters got saved and gave their life to Christ.

Saving souls is not so much about studying in theological seminaries or earning a lot of degrees. Instead, it is about sharing your testimony with the passion and burning love that Christ has given to you. Then you will see souls being saved into the kingdom. What about you? Do you have a testimony?

You Have a Testimony

Living testimonies are a great influence in bringing people to Christ. Explaining someone else's story will not be as powerful as telling your own experience. Unfortunately, many of us today do not share our testimonies in the manner in which it should be done. Sometimes this is because we do not see our own testimony as being as powerful as someone else's, or we underestimate our own story. This attitude should change. It does not matter how simple or childish your testimony might seem to others. Your testimony can change another person's life, no matter who that person may be.

Every testimony of salvation is created to bring some people to the Lord. The thing you need to do is share your testimony and discover who is meant to hear it! I believe with all my heart that if we Christians would just use our testimonies to reach out, then Christianity would grow at a much faster rate than it is growing today.

One of the problems we face is that we let the clergy do the work of sharing the Word of God. We depend too much on the pulpit. As a result, there are many spiritually fat Christians who know a lot, who experience a lot and who have a lot of testimonies, but are not sharing them. Women, youth and even children are a very powerful force for evangelism. If the born-again Christian women in the world would just share their testimony of Christ and the freedom He has given to women, I believe that there would be revivals among Muslim and Hindu women. How do we share our testimonies? There are two ways of sharing, verbally or through action.

VERBAL TESTIMONY

Verbal testimony is the story of your life, how you met Christ, and how Jesus entered your life and changed you. This can be through a healing, a dream, a vision, a conference or many other ways. One thing you must do is be open to the Holy Spirit and let His passion burn in your heart while you share your testimony with someone.

In other words, you must share it with love and the strength of the Holy Spirit and tell it as if it only happened yesterday. Many people grow cold in their love for Christ. They have forgotten the very day and the feelings they had when Jesus came into their lives. That same passion must be kept alive. Revelation 2:4 talks about the first love by saying, "Nevertheless I have this against you that you have left your first love." Verbal testimonies are impor-

tant in reaching souls. Many people, or at least a person, are out there waiting for your testimony. Share your testimony and then see the difference you can make.

TESTIMONY IN ACTION

Many people do not live out what they believe and do not practice what the Lord has asked them to do. Still we must have a desire to be holy or to live a life worthy of Christ. Jesus Christ was a great example of a testimony in action. While preaching forgiveness, He forgave people. His way of life showed that He truly was from God and the Savior of mankind. We Christians must put into practice what we believe, because that is a testimony by itself.

A testimony through action is powerful! Because Jesus did so, I will do the same; because God asked us in the Holy Bible, I will obey. When using verbal testimony or testifying in action, remember also that people will not always agree with you. People will despise and mock you for your testimony or beliefs, but this is a part of carrying the cross! For this reason you are born, to share your testimony with others around you so that you might at least bring one soul into the kingdom.

JUST A TASTE

The church in Cyprus and the miracles that took place there were just ladders in God's plan for my ministry. God always tests us in little things before

He gives us bigger ones. In the next chapter I will share with you the incredible miracles that took place and how God opened the doors for an international ministry. God is always interested in how we handle the assignments He gives us. Some people want to preach to a large group of people, yet they cannot even handle one person. Some people want to become a millionaire, yet they cannot handle the little money they have. Remember everything starts small. Every long journey starts with a little step.

Be faithful to whatever God has given you, whether it is small or big. The importance does not lie in the size of God's assignment. What really matters is a heart ready and willing to hear His voice.

Chapter 6

"Move"

After what happened in Cyprus, I traveled there regularly to encourage the people in the church. I never had any idea about God's plan for me at that time. In March 1997, the Lord said He wanted to use me for the world. I asked God, "How, Lord? I am a nobody. Besides that, there are already powerful preachers traveling around the world preaching the Word. Who is going to listen to me any way?"

The Lord said, "There is a 'Buy and Sell Newspaper' in which you can place advertisements free of charge in more than fifteen countries. Place an ad there and call people to partner with you. Send them your free cassettes and preaching videos and newsletters on a regular basis." The Lord further said that He wanted the poor. They almost never have the chance to receive the gospel on cassettes and video for free. He told me to place the ad and then wait.

Time passed, and by April, the first person who replied to our ads sent us a fax. She was from South Africa. Other replies came from different nations of Africa, where I never even placed any ads. We also received replies from nine other countries, so we sent the first shipment to them.

When I shared this with friends, they thought I was mad. Some people did not even take me seriously, but they did not know that God was behind this idea. Some asked, "Who is going to reply to you? Who is interested in your audio tapes? People know Benny Hinn and Reinhard Bonnke, but no one knows you." Deep in my heart I knew that this is not about a person, but rather that these men of God are vessels of the Spirit of God. If they are filled with the Spirit, then I am also filled with the same Spirit. The same Spirit that made Christ rise from the dead also abides in me. So, I did not pay attention to the discouraging words of people.

After receiving some positive reactions, I thought of putting one more ad in the same newspaper. But the ad never came through. I received a letter from the chairman of the newspaper who informed me that since I am advertising in the name of a church I must pay something like twenty dollars per city in which I want to advertise. I calculated that it would cost me around one thousand dollars to place the same ads that I had at first placed almost free of charge! I agreed to place the ad again and sent the money through the bank, but after a few days the money was returned to our account. I did not understand it.

I phoned the office of the newspaper and asked the man in charge of international advertisements. The gentleman said, "Dr. Lee, I know you! We have made a mistake. It is our policy never to place any Christian born-again ads in our international columns!"

I was shocked! I replied, "How in the world was that made possible? You placed the first series of our ads almost free of charge?" The man answered, "We made a mistake through human error," and he hung up the phone. *That was a miracle!* I believe that God confused the person who worked in that newspaper. Once we had placed the ads, they could not take it back. It was made possible not by might, nor by power, but by the Spirit of God—my Partner for life, my dearest Friend and Supporter. Moments come in our lives in which God takes control of and only needs our obedience. The Israelites never could have passed through the Jordan River if they had not first placed their feet in the water, or if they had never moved toward the Promised Land.

WORLD EVANGELISM

The months passed by, and in October 10, 1997, we had a prayer meeting in our church hall that was meant for only members of our team. We prayed that cold night, and suddenly, the presence of the Holy Spirit filled the room. All of my team members fell to the floor under the power of God, and we were all "drunk" in the Spirit and shaking. A little ball, which belonged to the Sunday school children, was in the room where we prayed. The Lord said, "Rise and take the ball in your both hands and hold it. This is the world. Take care of it. I will send you to the nations." At the same time three of our sisters saw a vision in which God placed a mantel on me that was called "World Evangelism." We went home at 4 A. M.

A day after the prayer meeting, I went to the post office to check the mail. First, there was an invitation from Swaziland. The Parliament of that nation and the prime minister were in the program. I opened another letter, which was an invitation from South Africa. They said they heard my sermons and were all touched by God. They wanted to join me in the movement of evangelism. Invitation after invitation came. The preaching cassettes we sent to the world brought revival even down into the prisons; people had been saved in groups.

The Holy Spirit came among them and moved right in the jails. Criminals came to Christ. Police officers came to Christ. Young people in different parts of the world were challenged in evangelism. God told me that if we wanted to reach the countries of the world, we must edify and anoint the natives and nationals with the power of Christ in order to train them and send them across the seas. From Australia to Europe and from Southern Africa to Asia, we were harvesting souls. From the highest ranked officers to the employees in government service to the poorest people in the world, people received, and are still receiving, the gospel free of charge.

In less than two years, mission centers were opened and pastors in various parts of the world left their traditional churches and joined the evangelism movements. Some were persecuted, rejected and even fired from their posts. They saw God's anointing and joined this fresh new movement.

However, the movement was not always acceptable to all believers, especially the leaders and elders. Once I traveled to Africa, and an elder paid people to take away our posters from the walls. He came to our meetings to observe and then go behind us to persecute us. One night during our conference, he was healed by the power of God! He came forward to share his testimony and to ask forgiveness from God. God is able; He is more than able!

Sometimes I am very amazed to see individuals in high ranks of the ministry come out to join and be used by God in this movement of fresh fire and anointing.

In less than three years, we were able to reach eighty nations of the world and impact these nations, groups and individuals for the gospel of Jesus Christ. I am also amazed at how young women and men who listen to the preaching cassettes get the fire and then travel through their towns and across their countries, saving souls. This evangelism movement is not the work of any man, but it is the work of a group of people joining hands together to reach the world with gospel of Christ through the power of the Holy Spirit. Only together are we strong!

WE HAVE IT ALL

One thing I have learned is that it is essential for everyone to know that money is not the only solution for churches and ministries to reach their goals in the Lord. Instead of money, human resources are essential for a successful ministry. I have seen ministries with huge amounts of money in their bank accounts, and yet they do not know how to use it because they do not have a team of people with loving hearts. They just freeze the work of God. Motivate a man and place him under the power of the Holy Spirit, and you will see fruit. The body of Christ does not need people hired by an organization for doing the job. We are not hired, we are bought! What we need are people with a calling who want to give their all for God's kingdom.

The Lord does not need only mega-churches in order to reach the world or to achieve God's plan here on earth. Small church, big church, famous evangelist or unknown evangelist, all of these do not matter as long as we realize that Christ is all we need.

Many times people ask me, "How do you do it? You

must have a lot of money." I always answer them with: "Christ and a powerful Spirit-filled team is all that I need." Remember, only twelve disciples in the beginning influenced the powers of the world.

TAKE THE STEP

One of the problems people deal with when they are starting out on something is that they put their focus on the obstacles they encounter along their way. Of course, we must be realistic in what we do, but if we only look at the barriers, we will be discouraged from starting something that God has called us to do—be it a ministry, a business, a family or whatever. Jesus has taught us that we must have the faith of a child.

Many people have come to my office and proposed to me their great dreams for a ministry. They know their calling and where they belong, but they do not take any action. Instead, they come to my office and ask me for a huge amount of money to start a ministry. They complain and suffer and wait until God moves for them. The secret, though, is that they must move first. Once I had a friend from Africa who moved from one ministry to another, complaining that no pastor wanted to accept him. Once he was an assistant to one pastor but switched to another pastor.

In less than a year he had already changed three churches. He had no job, no house and no residency papers to stay in the West. Deep in his heart, he knew he was supposed to be in Africa and in his own country; but he was not listening to God's voice. One day he came to my office and told me that he wanted to open a church in his city in Africa. I said to him, "Wonderful! You have come back to your senses. Now you know where you belong!"

He said, "But I need four thousand dollars immediately."

I was puzzled and said to him, "If you want the money immediately, then you also need to answer the call of God immediately." In addition I told him, "You have nothing here, no job, no proper house and no papers. Come with me now to the airport, and I will pay for your return ticket home so that you can go and start the work."

He jumped up and said, "First give me four thousand dollars."

I answered, "Not a penny. You must move and obey the call of God now. Then I will give you the money!" Jesus said in Matthew 6:33, "Seek first his kingdom and his righteousness, and all the things will be given to you."

An incredible story in the Bible is when Jesus walked on water during a storm, while His disciples were in a boat. The boat was nearly sinking. The disciples saw from afar a figure walking on the water and approaching them. Peter said, "If you are the Lord, call me to come to you." Jesus said to him, "Come to me, walk on the water." Peter walked for a while on water, but the minute he saw the waves coming at him, he took his eyes off of Jesus, and he began to sink. Jesus saved him and pulled him out of the water.

We may be like Peter. Instead of focusing on His call, we are focusing on the waves and the difficulties, which will be our fall and could cause us to do nothing. Proverbs 26:13 addresses this same idea by asking, "Why doesn't the lazy man ever get out of the house? What is he afraid of? Lions?"

Move toward the call of God and see Him bless you. He will be with you when you pass through the rivers and fires and will save you from your enemies. He will be with you when you pass through the valleys and the shadows of death. The only thing you need to do is to move and act.

Please understand that God doesn't expect you to make it at once. God does not expect you to become the greatest in what He has called you to do. No! What He wants you to do is to take the steps, even if you fall or fail. He wants you to move. That is your test!

Chapter 7

Soldiers of the Cross

A S YOU READ THIS CHAPTER, I WARN YOU TO GET READY. *I believe your life is going to change. The Holy Spirit is going to touch your heart and change your life in a radical way. You will experience God's power of the Pentecost once again, and God will prepare you for this greatest harvest of souls that is going to take place in this new millennium. Just get ready, open your heart and read this chapter carefully. No matter who you are, God wants to use you! I will discuss the world, the church and you. So fasten your seat belt and be ready to take off for this incredible journey!*

OUR WORLD IS SICK

Today our planet is carrying more than six billion

people. World population is growing like never before in the history of mankind. Such incredible growth has caused more wars, more killings, more crimes and more environmental disasters than ever before. Even animals are not spared because of the cruelty of the man's actions and choices.

Poverty is reaching its maximum, and the gap between the rich and poor is becoming wider. Only 20% of the world's population earns 85% of the incomes of the world. According to the 1995 statistics of the United Nations, the people in the West and Northern America are 150 times richer than people living in Third-World countries. I have received letters from pastors and church workers in India, Africa and the other parts of the world asking for support because they are dying of hunger. I just received a letter from a pastor in India who asked for support because he only earns fifty U.S. dollars a month! Can you imagine this?!

A reliable report from a country in Africa states that one out of six women has experienced violence and rape, directly or indirectly. Whole villages in Africa are dying of AIDS.

However, the West may actually be far worse than other parts of the world. In many parts of the world, people may be poor in material and physical aspects, but in the West people are poor in the spirit. They are surrounded by monetary wealth, but they need love. Instead of being loved by their spouses or children, people try to find love in animals by adopting dogs or cats. Of course, we are making some general observations here.

Immorality is increasing every day. Never before in history could we read so much about the meanness and rudeness of people. How many times do we hear about fathers abusing their children, or even mothers doing the same? How many times do we read in the news about a teenager getting a gun and shooting children at school? What about the thousands of unborn children who are killed daily through abortion? What about children who are kidnapped and killed, and their organs sold for huge amounts of money? How many times do husbands abuse their wives—beat them, rape them and even kill them? How many children today are left without a father or a mother because of family fights and divorce?

Surely the world is sick, but this is not God's fault! Many people blame God, but the fault is ours. We are messed up! Our choices have caused destruction. As I mentioned earlier, it is man's choices that have shaped our history. We cannot say it was God who killed six million Jews in the concentration camps. Not at all. It was the choice of those men in power at that time in history that allowed it to happen. Do not tell me that it was the choice of those little children and women in Algeria, Yugoslavia, Iraq or any other place in the world to be molested and murdered! No, not at all! God did not do these cruel things, but people did!

THE SOLUTION

What, then, is the solution for this sick world and for people who live in it? Many people believe that money is the solution. Some say, "If we give money to the poor nations, then they will come out of the poverty; or if we help them start their own businesses, then they will be helped." But, that is not the solution. If money were the solution, then we would not have the problems of today. In fact, the Bible teaches in 1 Timothy 6:10 that the love of money is a root of all evil. If the love of money is the source of all evil, then how can money be the source of help and blessing? Please do not misunderstand. I do not mean that money is bad. We need to give to the poor. What I am saying is that money is not the source of solution and blessing. Money can make some things easier, but it is not the solution.

Human beings have tried everything to solve the problems of the world, but it has not worked. You can see it for yourself; the world is not heaven! I still remember what my university professor said. "My son, you cannot change the world. I tried. My hair grew gray but I couldn't." Yes, my professor was right. We cannot change the world, but Jesus Christ can change the individuals who make up this world.

THE ROOT

Money, politics and loans could only partly solve the surface of the problems. We need a solution that heals the root. We cannot change the entire world, but we can change individual lives. I believe that the root of our problems in our world and society is in the hearts of the billions of individuals who inhabit our planet.

Individuals make history; they are participating in the process of making history. Individuals make up groups that represent their common interests and goals. We must work at the individual level. Change a man, and all his family will change! Change a woman, and all the children she is raising up will be influenced.

For example, there was a drunkard who beat his wife and children and who gambled every day. He got cancer and was dying. He went to the doctors but they could not heal him. Desperate, he found this man who was said to have healing powers. He was some sort of guru. The man visited him, and after going there for prayers, he got healed of cancer. In two months he was totally healed! But he continued beating his wife and children, and committing other evil acts. That man was healed only on the surface, not from the root. He was not changed at all. In other words, that healing was useless because there was no conviction of sin and repentance in the life of this man.

The world is made up of individuals and of personalities. The Bible tells us that all have sinned and fall short of the glory of God (Rom. 3:23). As I mentioned earlier, this sinful condition is a curse that entered the human race through the sin of Adam and Eve. That sin is rooted in us today; that sin has developed into various forms and shapes. Such sin must be uprooted out of a person's heart. I have always believed that sinful acts such as raping, killing, hate and anger are not sins on their own but are the side effects of a greater sin. You might ask, "What actually, is this greater sin?" Please do not be confused. *Sin is man's disobedience to God's voice, and His universal laws that He gave us through His prophets, all of which were fulfilled and accomplished in Jesus Christ Himself.* Sin started in Eden, and it continues today. God sent His Son, Jesus Christ, to this world, but this world rejected Him. This rejection of Jesus Christ as Lord and Savior by mankind is the sin of man. Sin brings side effects such as the acts I mentioned, but sin begins with disobedience to God. We are condemned when we reject Jesus Christ as Lord and Savior. And we are condemned when we ignore the laws of God in our lives, families, societies, business and countries.

How can sin be uprooted out of man? This can only happen when sinful man falls on his knees, repents and becomes born again. And this is only possible when we receive Jesus Christ as Lord and are filled with His Holy Spirit. This is only the first part of the new change. The other part must come by our own willingness to be disciplined and trained in God's kingdom in order to be a better person—a changed one! For God disciplines His beloved ones.

JESUS IS THE SOLUTION

Chapter three in the Book of Acts tells the story of a beggar sitting at the temple court for many years, asking for money. This man was paralyzed from birth. While on the way to the temple, Peter and John saw this man. The man thought Peter and John would give him money. But Peter said to him, "Silver or gold I do not have, but what I have I give you. In the name of Jesus Christ of Nazareth, walk" (v. 6).

Peter and John did not have any silver or gold, nor did they have medicine for the man's physical problem. But they had a name that could solve the man's main problem—his paralyzed legs. Only the name of Jesus could heal the beggar.

You may have tried to find solutions for problems in your family or yourself. I tell you this: There is nothing impossible when you mention the name of Jesus Christ with faith. And in His name, the gospel should be preached in all over the world—to the poor and to the rich, to the oppressed and to the oppressor, to families, cities and nations.

He was poured out for us as a medicine. He took our sins away and removed them by the root. Isaiah 53 says that He took our infirmities and sickness upon His shoulders; He healed us by His wounds. There is a powerful verse in the Bible that says, "Every knee should bow . . . every tongue should confess that Jesus Christ is Lord" (Phil. 2:11).

Who Knows the Name?

Six billion souls live in the world today. I believe more than 85 percent of the world's population have never heard the gospel of Jesus in the way it should be heard. Millions of people are born without Christ, live without Christ and die without Christ. What, then, is our role as Christians in our world? Are we born for nothing? Do we just practice Christian values among fellow Christians? What about the Great Commission Jesus has given to us?

If you are a Christian reading this, or you just became one, it is your duty to share the gospel with the people around you. Matthew 24:14 says, "And this gospel of the kingdom will be preached in the whole world as a testimony to all the nations, and then the end will come." Who shall preach the gospel as a testimony? You. God needs you!

You do not need to attend a six years of theological school and then get a pastorate degree and then be involved in an institution or organization in order to share your testimony. Please! If you want to preach theology, then study theology. I am not against it. Knowledge is good. But if you want to change someone's life by telling your testimony, you only need to open your mouth. Do not be ashamed of the gospel of Jesus Christ. Tell the whole world what Jesus Christ did for you.

You — the Bride of Christ

We are the bride of Jesus. (See Revelation 21:2, 9.) We are married to Jesus, figuratively, both as a church and as individuals. After God created the world, He saw that everything He made was good. But the Bible teaches us that there was only one thing in the eyes of God which was not good: The Lord God said, "It is not good for man to be alone. I will make a *helper* suitable for him" (Gen. 2:18, italic added).

The Lord caused the man to sleep, and while he was sleeping, God took one of the man's ribs and formed woman as a partner for man. She was called *woman,* because she was taken out of man. The word *woman* in the Hebrew language sounds similar to the word *man.* Out of the many things God has created, none of them was a suitable partner for Adam except the woman. Woman was called into existence because Adam needed a partner and a helper.

For centuries, in the Old Testament, God considered Israel as His own bride and holy nation. When the Second Adam (Jesus Christ) died on the cross, out of His wounds, a church was formed but not yet activated. And so, at Pentecost, God took this church and breathed into her the Holy Spirit and, from that day on, the church became His bride and His helper.

> *The church was made because Jesus needed a helper. It was not good for Jesus to be alone. Jesus wants to fulfill His divine plan on earth through the church, and you are part of that church. It is time for you to stand up. It is time for you to let those around you know that you have the Light of the world in you. Jesus had sent out His disciples to fulfill the Great Commission. Today He needs the disciples of this time. Who is worthy to be called a disciple? You, if you want it so!*

Christianity is far more than going to a Sunday worship service, listening to a preacher's messages and trying to live it out for the rest of the week. Christianity is about fulfilling God's purpose here on earth. God is interested in those who represent Him here on earth. It does not matter who these people are, whether they are educated or not, male or female, young or old, poor or rich. God wants to use everyone who loves Him and obeys His Word.

WHO ARE YOU?

Have you ever asked yourself this important question: "Who am I?" Go and look into a mirror. Who do you see? Do you see a person who is defeated, miserable, broken and useless? Or do you see a person full of potentials and a bright future in Christ Jesus? Who are you?

The Bible says that before we were even born, the Lord knew our names, He formed us and created us in our mothers' wombs. Even then, He had a plan prepared for us here on earth. But our Lord is a good Lord; He is a good and righteous God. He will never push His plans on you, unless you choose for His plans. So God's plans for you are the best that you can get and His plans are to use you so that His kingdom may come.

When the disciples of Jesus asked Him to teach them to pray, Jesus said,

This, then, is how you should pray:

"Our Father in heaven,
hallowed be your name,
your kingdom come,
your will be done on earth as it is in
heaven."
— MATTHEW 6:9–10

How can God's kingdom come here on earth? Through you! He wants to use you so that His kingdom may come. He is looking for you. No matter where you are, even in the prison, He can use you if you allow Him to do so.

Look at the world, the evil is controlling and influencing many souls. Look at how many people die from drugs, how many women are beaten by their husbands. Look also at the Internet and see how the devil has taken control of it. See the TV programs, full of violence and bloodshed. Go and walk around the dark sides of your town and see how many people are living on the rags of society. Read the newspapers and see how many children are abused and how many families have fallen apart.

What is the role of church? Church as a building will not be able to change the world. Church starts with you. You are a part of the church. God created you so that He could use you and make a hero of you, regardless of your gender or age.

Where are you now? Where did you end up? What do you want out of this life? You can not bring your money, your cars or your riches with you to the grave. What will you do with these things? What will people say about you, once you have gone to be with Lord? Will they remember you as a person who made a difference?

What do you want to be, a soldier of the cross, a hero of God or just a normal person like others?

Go now, look into the mirror once again. Who do you see? Let me tell you who you see: You see a potential hero, you see a child of God, you see someone who is ready to be used by God, now!

First Peter 2:9 says this:

> But you are chosen people, a royal priesthood, a holy nation, a people belonging to God, that you may declare the praises of Him who called you out of darkness into his wonderful light.

YOUR PURPOSE

It is time for you to challenge the devil and his kingdom! What do you do to give the devil restless hours? He is not shaken when you simply wash the dishes in your church or clean the preacher's desk. To threaten the devil's kingdom, you must know your purpose!

Jesus knew His purpose in coming to earth. John said, "The reason the Son of God appeared was to destroy the devil's work" (I Jn. 3:8). Your purpose is the same! Jesus commissioned every believer with His power and authority. (See Matthew 28:18, ff.). And He said that miraculous signs would accompany His believers: "In my name they will drive out demons; they will speak in new tongues; they will pick up snakes with their hands; and when they drink deadly poison, it will not hurt them at all; they will place their hands on sick people, and they will get well" (Mk. 16:17-18).

Of course, Jesus was not suggesting that we drink poison or handle snakes. He was saying that nothing of the devil will be able to harm us, because our purpose is to destroy the devil's kingdom by healing the sick, casting out demons and many other works. Until now, you may have thought that these are the works of a preacher or a pastor. No, not at all! Jesus was speaking about all believers, including you! You have received power and authority from Jesus Christ. He has given you the right to heal, to pray and to cast out demons. Exercise your authority!

Through your boldness in Christ and your aggressive prayers, people suffering in the grips of the devil can be set free and brought into God's kingdom. You can bring healing and salvation to your family, your neighborhood, your city and your country. You can even influence the course of history by knowing and fulfilling your purpose. You have the power; use it!

Chapter 8

The Last Word

WHEN I LOOK BACK AT MY LIFE THAT I HAVE SHARED in this book, it seems like a dream. Events pass through my mind just like in a movie. What a wonderful God I have and serve! I recall the man selling pictures of Jesus on the cross, and my school with the old-fashioned church inside the yard. I remember my grade-school friend who gave me the plastic cross. More than that, I remember the Lord's visitation in my hotel room in Spain and His audible words, "I am knocking at the door . . ." All of these experiences have not only drastically impacted my own life, but also the lives of thousands of people who have crossed my path in my ministry.

My past experiences, and all that is to come, are challenging me to continue this journey in the power and anointing of my best Friend, the Holy Spirit. He stands by my side to support me. I am no longer a little boy carrying a plastic cross. Every morning when I wake up, I take my real "cross" just like a soldier and carry it with me. Today I am not a soldier of a plastic cross, but a soldier of the cross!

> *God wants radical Christians, Christians who know no boundaries and limits in God's kingdom. You can make a difference if you want, if you take yourself and the commitments you have received seriously enough. You can do it by serving the Lord with all your godly passion and love for Jesus Christ. Read what Jesus said,*
>
> *I am the true vine and my Father is the gardener. He cuts off every branch in me that bears no fruit, while every branch that does bear fruit, he prunes so that it will be even more fruitful. You are already clean because of the word I have spoken to you. Remain in me and I remain in you. No branch can bear fruit by itself; it must remain in the vine. Neither can you bear fruit unless you remain in me.*
> *—JOHN 15:1–4*
>
> *He further said:*
>
> *You did not choose me but I chose you and appointed you to go and bear fruit—fruit that will last.*
> *—JOHN 15:16*
>
> *Remember there are souls waiting for your testimony: Don't forget, someone is knocking at the door.*
> *He wants to use you! Open the door! Start the day now! Seize the day! Don't be just a Christian, but be a hero, a Soldier of the Cross!*

*For more information or to schedule Dr. Lee
for ministry engagements, contact:*

JESUS CHRIST FOUNDATION WORLD EVANGELISM
P.O. Box 12429
1100 AK Amsterdam
The Netherlands

Phone: +31-20-6994897 / 6610818
Fax: +31-20-4167309

Visit our website at:
www.slwe.org